Acting with Power

Acting with Power

Why We Are More Powerful
Than We Believe

DEBORAH GRUENFELD

Currency | New York

CURRENCY and its colophon are trademarks of
Penguin Random House LLC.

LIBRARY OF CONGRESS CATALOGING-IN-PUBLICATION DATA
Names: Gruenfeld, Deborah H, author.
Title: Acting with power / Deborah Gruenfeld.
Description: First edition. | New York: Currency, [2019] | Includes index.
Identifiers: LCCN 2019030218 (print) | LCCN 2019030219 (ebook) |
ISBN 9781101903957 (hardcover) | ISBN 9781101903964 (ebook)
Subjects: LCSH: Power (Social sciences) | Authority. |
Leadership. | Role playing.
Classification: LCC HM1256 .G77 2019 (print) |
LCC HM1256 (ebook) | DDC 303.3—dc23
LC record available at https://lccn.loc.gov/2019030218
LC ebook record available at https://lccn.loc.gov/2019030219

Hardback ISBN 978-1-101-90395-7
International ISBN 978-0-593-13868-7
Ebook ISBN 978-1-101-90396-4

Printed in the United States of America on acid-free paper

randomhousebooks.com

2 4 6 8 9 7 5 3 1

First Edition

Book design by Virginia Norey

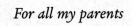

For all my parents

Contents

Acting with Power

Introduction

The Problem with Power

I found this drawing in the farthest reaches of a file drawer at my mother's house. I knew right away who it was. The person has too many eyes, a closed mouth, and no real arms or hands. She sees everything but can't act on what she knows. It's me, in my first self-portrait, drawn when I was three.

Looking at me now, the resemblance may not be obvious. I'm a chaired professor at Stanford University who has been studying, writing, and teaching about the psychology of power for over twenty-five years. I have an exciting career. I have a voice and I know how to use it. Today, the first self-portraits of my own children are stashed somewhere in the farthest reaches of a file drawer in *my* house. A lot has changed since I was three, but that little stick-person is definitely still with me.

There was a time when I thought it was just me who felt this way. But if I've learned anything in my work on power, it's that I am not alone. Everyone feels powerless sometimes, no matter how much power they have. And we all have power, whether we can realize it or not.

It's not intuitive. But the idea of power can make us feel small. In part, it's that we learn about power in childhood, at a time in our lives when we are at our most vulnerable, and the association lingers. The first power-holders we meet—that is to say, our parents and other adult caretakers—teach us lessons about how to survive in the family that most of us never outgrow. We all come into adult relationships with childhood baggage—insecurities, habits, and comfort zones that draw us into old, familiar dramas where we can play old, familiar roles. The first brush with power leaves an indelible mark.

As an academic, I've written a lot about what having power might be like, and as a person, I've hoped against hope that becoming an expert and attaining stature in my field would help me feel more powerful and make it easier for me to be me. Yet having power, to the extent that I do, has not felt like I thought it would. Power attracts attention, and greater scrutiny. Higher expectations, and more ways to fail, with more at stake. Having power has done little to relieve me of my childhood insecurities. It has just provided a bigger stage on which to act them out.

Learning to Play the Professor

Becoming a professor was a fairly dramatic transition. I was a graduate student for five long years, so that role had become quite comfortable. I got my PhD and accepted a job at Northwestern University, and on my very first day, just like that, became "the professor." I still felt like the same person, doing the same work—running experiments, publishing journal articles, and learning to teach—but to everyone else I was different. I was supposed to know things, to be the expert, to hold other people accountable and tell my students what to do.

It was the most uncomfortable of ironies. As a psychologist, I was a bona fide power expert. But I still felt powerless myself. I felt like an imposter, undeserving of the respect and attention that come with the role. And the more I advanced in my career, and the more my stature grew, the more I struggled to own who I was to other people. I could see how others looked in positions of power; I just couldn't see myself as one of them.

Then I had a breakthrough. It came from an unexpected place. I was asked to take part in a new program being offered to business school faculty in an effort to increase teaching quality across the board. The program was offered by a consultant whose background was in the theater. It seemed a little woo-woo, even for California, but I agreed to participate because, true to form, I thought I had to.

I spent two full days in a claustrophobic lecture hall with eight other faculty members and a diminutive, supercharged woman named Barbara Lanebrown. She asked each of us to prepare three minutes of a typical lecture and deliver it to our colleagues. After the first presentation, she asked the speaker—a gray-haired expert in international business with a British accent—an unexpected question:

"Which characters," she asked, "did you bring with you onto the stage?" He blinked at her, genuinely puzzled, until finally, one colleague, sensing his discomfort, asked Lanebrown to clarify. A classroom, she explained gently, "is like a theater, where we play the role of teacher." Then she paused to let that sink in. "When we give a lecture," she continued, "we are giving a performance. Like an actor, we make choices about how to play that role by enlisting characters that live within us who help us bring it to life."

Some of us shifted and smiled weakly, and I thought I heard someone snort. I remember looking around to see if anyone was buying it. Then someone voiced what I was feeling: "I don't act in the classroom. I'm just being myself."

Lanebrown considered this comment. Then she asked us about the teaching presentation we'd just seen. Was this person, whom you know as a colleague but have never seen teach, different at all in the role of teacher? Did you see a side of him you hadn't seen before, or learn anything about him that you weren't aware of?

The answer, of course, was yes. "Onstage" he wasn't exactly the same as the person we knew outside the classroom. As each person delivered their three-minute spiel, this proved to be true again and again. One guy, generally your typical buttoned-up academic, became more of "a stand-up comic." Another normally easygoing and unusually friendly colleague became more stern, even a bit scary; he described himself, aptly, as "the sheriff." A third, who was somewhat impulsive and feisty in faculty meetings, took on the quiet gravitas of "the village elder." Every single one of us revealed a hidden side of ourselves when teaching. We each drew, however unconsciously, on characters we knew, who lived in us already, to give our best, or at least most comfortable, performance.

It was completely eye-opening. I learned that I brought an army of characters with me to deliver my lecture: the energetic one, the passionate one, the nervous one, the playful one, the vulnerable one, the intellectual one, the knowledgeable one, the serious one, the articulate one, and the powerful one. Needless to say, not all were actually invited, but they made their appearances anyway, and apparently the stage wasn't big enough for the ten of us. I didn't really trust any of them, it turned out: I feared that the strong ones would be off-putting and the weak ones would be pitiful. The result was that they were all wrestling behind the curtain, and the audience could see it.

Each of us left the room that day with an assignment: to prepare another few minutes of lecture, but this time to try to commit to showing up in character more. We arrived on Day Two ready for a challenge. Some took bigger risks than others. The village elder came in slightly more rumpled, with a folksier way of speaking. The sheriff wore cowboy boots and, on occasion, used his fingers as guns, to great effect. I can't recall what I tried to do, which is telling.

But what I do remember is that, unlike some of my colleagues, I couldn't stop self-censoring. And at the same time, I could see that when my colleagues were able to let go of being themselves and fully embrace the roles they were playing, their performances actually became more compelling, more engaging, more "true." Somehow, acting didn't make them seem less "authentic"; it actually made them appear more real.

*

I now know that power is not personal, at least not in the way I once thought. In life, as in the theater, power comes with the roles we play. Actors, if they are successful, don't let their insecurities stop them from being who they need to be in order to do their jobs. To do any job well, to be the person you aspire to be, and to use power effectively (whether you feel powerful or not), you have to step away from your own drama and learn how to play your part in someone else's story.

I might feel unsure of myself as "the professor," but that is, in fact, who I am. For me, acting as the professor is not "faking it"; it is accepting a shared social reality and committing to play my part.

We don't always feel comfortable with the idea of ourselves as power-holders. But to use power well, we have to bring out the best part of ourselves at the right moments, while keeping the more insecure, less useful parts tucked away. Or, in the words of the great Judi Dench, "The trick is to take the work seriously, but not take yourself seriously at all."

Being Cast as the Femme Fatale

In 2015, on the first day of classes, I found myself in the news. A tenured professor had been caught in a "love triangle" between her estranged husband and the dean of the Graduate School of Business, where all three of them happened to work. The story got a lot of attention. Reporters from *The New York Times, The Wall Street Journal,* and *Businessweek,* among other outlets, had access to personal correspondence—the most personal kind you can imagine—between the dean and the professor, and were calling around for comment.

This was not a role I aspired to play. I was the butt of a joke: an expert on power and misconduct who was, according to initial reports, having "a secret affair" with her boss. Never mind the facts: that we were both single, that we had been dating for almost three years, and that the relationship was not a secret. Or that we had followed university policy, thinking that was enough. The fact that I was involved with "The Dean" changed the optics. The story of our relationship became high drama, with me cast as "the femme fatale."

As an expert on power, you would think I might have seen it coming, and that I should have known how it might look. But before the story broke, I still had an arm's-length relationship to power. I had studied it, thought about it, taught about it. Before that day, I had played with power, like a toy in a sandbox. Turned it over and pushed it around, to see how it worked. For my entire adult life, I had found power fascinating. But I couldn't see what it had to do with me.

The first big shock when the news broke was that anyone cared. In my mind, we were two private, newly single, middle-aged people who had found each other and were being given a second chance at love. Our world became very small. We spent a lot of time worrying about our kids and how they would handle our relationship. We did not think it would matter to anyone else. Of course, we were wrong. Our world felt small, but the stage we were standing on wasn't.

The femme-fatale thing blew over. Today I know I am not a caricature. And I know that although I can't control how other people see me, what other people say about me does not define who I am. Today I see myself as an actor would: as a person who is messier and more real. I am that character who tries her best but still makes mistakes, who is caring but also has needs, who is confident and yet has insecurities, who is powerful in some ways but powerless in others, and who takes her responsibilities seriously but plays her roles imperfectly.

In the theater, what it means to give a powerful performance is to accept and own the truth of what it means to be a human being: to be strong and weak, accomplished and fallible, powerful and powerless, all at once. This, actually, is the challenge that professional actors face every time they get in character. To play any part authentically, an actor must accept the character without judgment. And this is true for the rest of us as well. By accepting that each of us is all of these things, by learning to value all of these truths and show all of these sides of ourselves when appropriate, and by handling our mistakes with grace and equanimity, we become more resilient, less ruled by shame and self-loathing, and, ultimately, more powerful. Ironically, this is where authenticity comes from: not trying to be more yourself, but learning to accept more of yourself.

For my part, I've come through the fire of my public embarrassment a much stronger person. I have witnessed that chilling deer-in-the-headlights look in strangers' eyes when they realize I'm the person they have read about. My response now is to focus on trying to make them more comfortable. Because I'm still doing what I love, trying to make myself useful, and playing the role that defines me as a person. And you know what? I'm not afraid of anything anymore. That, more than anything, is how I know that I have all the power I need.

We aren't always cast in the roles we desire, or in roles we feel prepared to play. But the show, as they say, must go on.

Becoming an Author

I am not the first writer to care about power. As a culture, we are obsessed with power—our own and everyone else's. There are a lot of books, and almost as many perspectives, on how to get more power. But for me, this approach misses the point. The one clear implication of all my research, and all my experience, both personal and professional, is that success, impact, and life satisfaction are not the result of how much power you can accumulate, or even how powerful others think you are; they are the result of what you are able to do for others with the power you already have.

This truth is unspoken in the current discourse on power, and the results are evident in every realm of social life. When we spend all of our time worrying about the power we don't have, we think of power as a resource for personal consumption and self-aggrandizement. We define the acquisition of power as an end in itself. We buy into the myth that we all need more power to reach our goals in life, and that how much power we have defines our worth as human beings. We accept that we should strive to attain the highest possible position whatever it takes, and maintain the upper hand in every circumstance. The traditional take on power teaches us that the key to success is to attain more power, faster, by whatever means necessary, and that the person with more power wins.

These assumptions are not just wrong much of the time. It is far worse than that. The idea that we all need more power plays into our worst fears about ourselves and heightens our most destructive instincts. When power-holders feel more powerless than they are, when they are out of touch with the reality of their circumstances, when they fear they have less power than they do, they become self-protective and incapable of generosity. We all know what it means to use power badly; just take a look at the news: hate-spewing world leaders, corrupt politicians, unscrupulous CEOs, sexually aggressive entertainment moguls, wealthy parents who cheat their kids' way through the college admissions game—the list goes on. People who use the power they have to manage their own powerless feelings are bound to stray from their responsibilities. This is what it means to use power badly.

What is less obvious is what it means to use power well; this is much more mysterious. The key, I believe, is accepting the reality that more often than not, we have more power than we think we do. It is not so far-fetched. Power exists in every role, and in every relationship; it's a resource that flows between people who need one another. And because relationship partners, by definition, both need one another and have something to offer, power is almost never absolute. This means that all of us—regardless of who we are, how much we stand out, or how well we fit in, and despite how we feel—have power by virtue of the roles we play in others' lives. To use power well, we need to think about power differently. We need to accept responsibility for the power we have. We need to take our roles and responsibilities more seriously than we do. That is why I'm writing this book.

The notion that we have more power than we think is probably disorienting. The idea that the roles and responsibilities that connect us to others might be a source of power, rather than just a source of weakness or constraint, sounds practically un-American, even to me. And the suggestion that looking out for number one might not lead most efficiently to the number one position probably sounds just plain wrong. But social science tells us that all of these things are true. It is not just personal agency, competitiveness, and a dog-eat-dog approach to social life that explains who attains the highest ranks in groups. To the contrary, research shows that across many species, individuals are rewarded with status (respect, admiration, and often more power) for using whatever strengths they have responsibly—by making themselves useful and solving group problems rather than just putting themselves first. There's nothing wrong with having personal ambitions or wanting to protect your own position. But we can also enhance our own standing in groups by caring, authentically, about those who are less powerful than we are. This is what it means to use power well.

This book seeks to correct common misconceptions about power: what it is, how it works, and how it affects every aspect of social life. It is informed by more than twenty years of scientific research on the psychology of power, and by my own experiences as both teacher and student in the classroom and elsewhere. It draws on the questions, stories, and wisdom of countless MBA students, executives, entrepreneurs, academics, professional actors, and leaders with whom I have talked, and from whom I have learned, about the true nature of power. And it distills the key lessons from an MBA course that began as a quirky experiment and quickly became one of the most oversubscribed electives at the Stanford GSB. The course teaches that true, lasting power comes not from chasing personal stature or attaching ourselves to powerful others. It comes from learning to see power, and leadership, as opportunities to advance a shared plotline.

✳

Acting with Power is a book about power for anyone who has ever felt powerless, whether in a position of power or not. It's for anyone who has felt apprehensive about stepping into a bigger role, and for any-one who has felt stuck in a smaller one. It's for anyone who wants to act with confidence while feeling insecure, or to own a role while feeling like an imposter. It's for anyone who wields power often but feels they could do it better.

It is for everyone who struggles with how to use power differently while still being oneself—both those who struggle to step up and be taken more seriously, and those who struggle to stand back and be less intimidating; it's for those who are used to hearing they are too aggressive, and those who have been told they are too nice.

It's for those who want to understand why some people abuse their power, and want to learn how to resist, to survive—or better yet, come out stronger. It's for people who have made mistakes with their power in the past and who aspire to master their demons. And it's for leaders striving to create cultures and environments where power is used responsibly and where bullying, harassment, and other abuses of power are unlikely; where the people in leadership roles are the right people, cast for the right reasons and rewarded for the right actions: people who take the responsibility of being a role model to heart.

The book is divided into four parts. Part One exposes common myths about power and looks at how power actually works, and how it doesn't. It defines what it means to act with power, and what it means to do it well. In Part Two, we'll look at why roles matter in social and professional life, especially when it comes to power; how to figure out the role in which you've been cast; and how to play that role better, whether it feels natural to you or not. We'll look at how past roles follow us into new situations and why some of us seem able to use power only one way. To use power well, we need to master both command-and-control and respect-and-connect approaches. So in Part Two we'll look at how to expand your range: how to get comfortable with both commanding when your instinct is to connect, and respecting when your instinct is to control.

Part Three examines how to manage the insecurities—what actors think of as performance anxiety—that naturally arise when we step onto a larger stage. We'll look at the challenge of role transitions, why the ability to change roles is so important, and how an actor might approach internalizing a new role that feels unfamiliar, to avoid "losing the plot." And we'll explain how it's possible to take roles seriously and still be yourself.

Part Four addresses abuses of power—like sexual aggression and bullying—and explains why they happen (it isn't always for the reasons you'd think). We'll look at how to avoid being cast as the victim or, inadvertently, as the villain; and how to avoid harming relationships in ways we do not intend. We'll look at how to play an active part in the drama that unfolds around us, rather than playing the bystander. Finally, we'll look at how power can be used at the top of an organization to create environments where abuses of power are less common than they currently seem to be.

Acting with Power is an approach to being powerful that places responsibility ahead of dominance, and maturity ahead of authenticity. It is a book about how to use power better by thinking less about yourself and staying focused on your context. And if you are anything like me or the people I work with, I think you'll find that this approach to social life can change everything: not just your comfort with authority, the quality of your relationships, and your success and impact in all kinds of roles, but also the functioning of groups you are a part of. When individuals stay focused on collective outcomes, on elevating one another's performances, it creates psychological safety, enhances agility and flexibility, and minimizes status and power contests so that energy can be channeled toward group goals. And, at the risk of sounding grandiose, I believe that more people acting with power can benefit society as a whole. By learning how to use power better and on a larger scale, we are better equipped to prevent the abuses of power that can make all kinds of social institutions toxic.

Most books on power are about winning battles with other people. This one is about winning battles with ourselves.

PART I

When the Curtain Goes Up

1

The Truth About Power

What It Is, What It Isn't, and Why It Matters

P ower is a captivating topic. No matter who I'm with—women or men, the 1 percent or the 99 percent, nonprofit managers or business leaders, entrepreneurs, middle managers, or senior executives—everyone cares about power, and for good reason: people in positions of power control our fates. Power attracts and repels. Power creates and destroys. Power opens doors and closes them. Power explains who goes to war, why there is peace, and what we fight about. Power dictates how we live and under what laws, who has material advantage and who doesn't. Bertrand Russell said that power is the fundamental force in human relations. As immortalized in the musical *Hamilton,* power determines who lives, who dies, and who tells your story.

Human interest in power has deep existential roots. Psychologists believe we care about power because we fear death, and power promises a kind of immortality. That may seem a bit heavy, but it makes evolutionary sense. Power has survival value. Power affords not just greater access to shared resources and control of our own outcomes but also greater connection to others and elevated status within the clan. Human psychology has evolved to support these evolutionary realities. With more power, we imagine, we can live longer, better lives and even live on in others' hearts and minds after we are no longer physically present.

We seek power often without knowing it. And as much as we hate to admit it, power contests are everywhere, even in places where we think they don't belong. Not just at work but at home, in our marriages, with our siblings, in our friend groups, and in society more broadly, power is a central organizing force. We are dealing with power differences and negotiating power all the time, often while we think we are doing other things.

When you start to pay attention, you can see these contests everywhere. While engaged in friendly conversations about topics other than power—the news, your teenager's curfew, even which restaurant to go to on date night—we are often really haggling about who knows more, who is better connected, whose interests matter most, who gets to be the decider, who holds the moral high ground, and who makes the rules.

Much has been written about the powerful—their habits, strategies, and foibles—and many have approached the study of power by looking up, with some combination of fear, admiration, and envy. This "cult of personality" approach seems to suggest that power resides in the person, someone who possesses a combination of superior charm and ruthless ambition that the rest of us don't. It implies that to be powerful means to pursue self-aggrandizement and world domination, at the expense of everything and everyone else. And so the rest of us, who find this approach to social life abnormal, if not distasteful, conclude that power is not for us. We step away. We cede control to be polite and distinguish ourselves from the bad guys. In effect, we hand our power over to the wrong people because we can't see how to be powerful ourselves and be a good person at the same time.

When I began to study power, the topic itself made me queasy. Like many of my generation, who grew up during the civil rights era, I was raised to care about social justice, to recognize unfairness in social life, and to believe in equal rights for all people. My first heroes were Martin Luther King, Jr., Bobby Kennedy, and my high school English teacher, who was a not-so-closet feminist. To be a good person, I thought, meant to reject power in all its forms.

So as a researcher, I set out to take some of the shine off power, to lift the veil and show the dark side. It wasn't hard to do. In study after study, in all kinds of tasks, we found that people we had randomly assigned to our "high-power" conditions were more impulsive, less self-conscious, and less attentive to the consequences of their actions than those we had assigned to "low-power" conditions. It seemed—at first—that power could bring out the villain in anyone.

But as the science evolved and more researchers caught the wave, the picture became more nuanced. Sometimes, when my colleagues and I placed normal people in positions of power in the lab, they became more self-serving and more oblivious to social norms. And other times, it was the opposite. Power didn't turn everyone into a monster; in fact, sometimes it brought out people's most cooperative, most prosocial instincts.

In our competitive culture, it is natural to think of power as a means of self-enhancement. But power is also a tool we can use to take care of the people we care about. And this in and of itself can also be self-enhancing. In fact, studies find that when people take personal risks by sacrificing more—sometimes doing more work rather than less, and sometimes investing their own resources in others with no promise of a return—their status in those contexts rises.

Over time, the picture has become clearer: **power makes people more likely to act on both their best and their worst instincts.** We all have self-serving impulses, but we are also all capable of putting the welfare of others first. The truth about power, I've come to realize, is not that power itself is inherently good or bad, or that those who have power are inherently superior or flawed. Rather, how we act with power depends on what is on our minds when the opportunities to use power arise. In the end, it is not how much power we have but what we do with it that defines who we are and our impact on the world.

What Is Power?

The concept of power can be confusing. What *is* power, exactly? It's important to spend a moment on this. Some people are content to know power when they see it. But if you want to predict who gets power, why, and how, you have to understand what exactly power is, and also what it isn't. As social psychologist Kurt Lewin famously pointed out, "There is nothing so practical as a good theory." If you want to deal effectively with power differences, change the balance of power, or even just figure out how much power you have in a particular situation, you have to know what power is and where it comes from.

Power, by definition, is the capacity to control other people and their outcomes. So your power comes from the extent to which others need *you, in particular,* for access to valued rewards, and to avoid punishments. When someone needs you for these things, you have more power over them than you would if other people could also meet their needs. When others need you, they are motivated to please you, and this gives you control.

Power is not status. Status is a measure of respect and esteem in others' eyes. Power and status are related, of course, but it is possible to have power without status. For example, when you are running late, and a stranger is leaving the only available parking space for blocks, the urgency of your situation and their ability to control the outcome—they could make you wait while they take a phone call— gives them power, whether they realize it or not. When you have status, you typically have power, because people want to be associated with you.

Power is not authority either. But these are also related. Authority is the right to tell others what to do based on a formal position or title. So authority and power mutually reinforce each other, but it is possible to have power without formal authority (as with the driver vacating the parking spot). It is also possible to have formal authority but no real power: for example, when a university administrator must approve or deny requests for additional research and travel funds but has no direct control over the budget.

Power and influence are also different. Influence is *the effect of* power. Some people prefer the idea of having influence over the idea of having power, because having influence implies you don't have to use force. But this is a false distinction. When you have the ability to force someone's hand, truly, you almost never have to use it.

In short, power is the capacity for social control. So that part is fairly simple, but it is also the tip of the iceberg. To use power effectively, we need to also understand how it works. Our beliefs and assumptions about the rules of power affect how we use it, and much of what we think about the rules is just wrong. In order to use power better, we need to start thinking about it differently. We need to start looking at power on the ground where it lives, in relationships, groups, organizations, and communities. Power is not a personal attribute or possession. Power is a part you play in someone else's story.

Why Power Isn't Personal

Myth: Power is personal; either you have it or you don't.
Truth: Power is social; it lives and dies in the context.

In our culture of individualism, we think power, like everything else, is personal. We treat it like an individual attribute, a possession, to acquire or accumulate. But if you look carefully at power, you can see how we've missed the big picture.

Power is not an aspect of the self; it cannot be possessed by a person. Wealth, fame, charisma, good looks, ambition, and self-confidence are all personal qualities we equate with having power. But these are merely potential *sources of* power. They may also be consequences of power. But none of these qualities guarantee leverage over other people.

What makes someone powerful—what makes others willing to comply with their wishes—is the degree to which they are needed. Any person's power depends entirely on the context in which power is being negotiated. Power lives and dies in relationships, in goals and objectives, in settings, and in social roles. For example, self-confidence is not a source of advantage in a context where everyone is self-confident, nor do good looks confer the same kind of social advantage among the other beautiful people as in contexts where one is the most attractive person in the room. And qualities like wealth, ambition, and fame are also completely relative. This idea that power is attached to some fixed set of characteristics or traits is a fundamental misunderstanding and has led to a lot of beliefs about power that just aren't true.

Power isn't permanent. It doesn't exist in fixed quantities. Rather, it is the result of an agreement between people about who has control in the relationship, over what, and when, based on who needs who more at the time. And this means you can't always take power with you from one scenario to another. A CEO who has power in a meeting with her direct reports, for example, does not necessarily have power in a meeting with her board, or at the dinner table with her teenagers.

Another way that power can be fleeting is that it corresponds to who adds more value in a particular context—a unique source of knowledge or skill is more powerful than a redundant source of knowledge or skill. And power corresponds to the strength of your allies, and the strength of your options, in the context of a particular relationship. A person with no allies and no alternatives is much less powerful than a person with the exact same competence and skill sets who has strong, committed relationships with people who can open doors.

Power is part of a social contract. People have power to the extent that others consent to being controlled. When powerful individuals violate the terms of the implicit agreements that give them power, they rarely stay in power for long. People leave abusive marriages, and children grow up and cut off their parents. A boss who repeatedly mistreats employees can eventually be fired, and a brutal dictator who incites enough moral outrage can provoke a revolution. The balance of power, in other words, can shift.

It's easy to see how a person could be the most powerful person in the room one minute and totally powerless another. An athlete might be powerful in the next draft after helping his team win the championship, but powerless after he busts up his knee during preseason training. A politician with a high approval rating might be powerful while she's in office, but powerless after she is caught with her hand in the coffer and forced to resign. And, although it probably goes without saying at this point, an entertainment mogul who wields his power to extract sexual favors from aspiring actresses is no longer powerful once no actors, directors, or investors will work with him.

Power is not a feeling. Feeling empowered or disempowered is one thing, but when it comes to assessing our own power, we are often badly miscalibrated. In the same way that feeling powerful does not mean you have power, feeling powerless doesn't mean that you are. When we let our feelings guide our actions, things rarely go as planned.

It's true that overestimating our power can sometimes have short-term benefits, especially when others also benefit from our bold actions. And underestimating our own power may seem like a mark of humility or modesty, both generally desirable traits. But in fact, it is much better to be able to see the reality of your circumstances for what it is. Failing to appreciate that others outrank us is the source of many faux pas. And failing to internalize our own power over others can have serious consequences as well. Sexual misconduct at work, for example, is in part attributed to the tendency of many bosses to underestimate the impact of their power on others. As an HR executive at a large telecommunications firm once disclosed, when confronted with complaints by female subordinates, many male executives are shocked. "What's the problem?" they ask. "She's a grown-up, she could have said no." But this misunderstands the reality of the subordinates' relationship to those in charge. By denying the truth of power differences, we create an unfair and potentially dangerous situation for everyone.

Power is not a right. Despite what some powerful people may believe, occupying a position of power doesn't automatically entitle anyone to respect or social control. When power is used poorly—to cheat the system from which it arose, or to achieve personal gain without regard for the group's welfare—power-holders lose status and legitimacy, and in some degree the ability to control others' outcomes. This happens all the time in countries where a crumbling, often corrupt, regime is struggling to maintain power against the will of an angry populace. Without status, illegitimate power-holders must resort to bullying, intimidation, and the use of force to maintain the upper hand. In general, the more someone has to show they are powerful, the less power they probably have.

Power is not (just) about appearances. But how we behave can make a difference. Just as we are terrible judges of our own power, we are easily misled about the extent to which others are powerful. This is in large part because power is not directly observable; it has hidden properties. We tend to see power more in certain kinds of people than others and to assume that these kinds of people are better suited for powerful roles. But when we attempt to infer who has power based on appearances, it is easy to make a mistake.

For example, a meek job candidate with a better offer is more powerful than an overconfident candidate with no concrete options. An entry-level employee with strong connections to powerful people in the firm can be more powerful than coworkers who rank higher or have been there longer. And an administrative assistant who controls access to the CEO's calendar can be the most powerful person in the organization (as many have learned the hard way). Knowledge is almost always a source of power, and you can't see directly what, or who, other people know.

Physical appearances can be suggestive of power—through the use of dominant body language, for example—but this too can be misleading. Animals display aggression when they feel threatened: that is, not when they are sure they can win, but when they fear they may lose. And there is some truth to what they say about people who drive fast, expensive cars and who strut around with swagger, who talk too much or laugh louder than anyone else, who flaunt wealth or status: often they are compensating for the feeling that they are not powerful enough in some other way. In fact, the most important person in the room is often the one who tries to appear unassuming, to avoid intimidating others or attracting unwanted attention.

You may feel more powerful after posing in the mirror, and you can sometimes win a power contest by bluffing, but what really matters in the long run is the truth, that is, the shared realities of the context in which you are operating.

Why Power Doesn't Have to Be Hostile

Myth: Power is about control.
Truth: Power is about control and connection.

The use of power is often associated with dominance and coercion, or the idea of forcing people to do things against their will out of fear. But power is not just the ability to threaten others with the use of force. Power is a source of social leverage that can be wielded, acquired, and invested in many far less aggressive ways. And in spite of its reputation in some circles, power doesn't just drive a wedge between people; it can also align people and bring them together.

Not only are less powerful people drawn to more powerful people, but powerful people are also often drawn to the less powerful; research on the "complementarity principle" shows this clearly. In this way, power differences are a force of attraction; they provide a structure for coordination and connection that creates and strengthens relationships. Hierarchical relationships can make it possible for people working together to accomplish shared goals efficiently, because they don't have to fight for control. So trying to use power without connection can be a waste of energy. As one experienced executive I know likes to say: "If you're leading and no one is following, you're just taking a walk."

According to the late Harvard psychologist David McClelland, an expert on power and human motivation, most professional adults describe their own challenges with power as a desire to be more assertive. But what we often fail to realize is that the ability to show respect and even submission can also be a source of power. Deference is treating another person in ways that acknowledge that their expertise and experiences are at least as important as your own. It does not mean you have less power than the person you are deferring to. It means you do not intend to use the power you have against your relationship partner. Deference is disarming, it signals an absence of threat, and it creates a foundation of trust that allows a relationship to form.

We earn status—respect, esteem, and high social rank in groups— by doing things that help the group function and move forward. When used well, a deferential approach to using power can be a source of status (and more power in the long run) because it is perceived as generous: it can help improve the quality of group decisions, can make others feel valued, and is important for earning others' trust.

In 1990, political scientist Joseph Nye introduced the concepts of hard power and soft power to the world of international affairs. *Hard power*, as he defined it, includes intimidation, military interventions, and coercive diplomacy, including the use of economic sanctions. *Soft power* is more like charm, negotiation, and the use of almost every other diplomatic tool that a country has at its disposal to align another nation's interests with its own. For decades, Nye argued, Americans had relied too much on hard power, and this undermined our national interests. At the time, China, whose great charm offensive had built alliances that led to the peaceful rise of a long-struggling country, was a shining example of how soft power can be used in combination with other tactics. Its leaders had leveraged the soft power of diplomacy as well as the building of cultural bridges and forging of business partnerships to achieve a position of strategic advantage.

Nye coined the term *smart power* to describe an approach to foreign policy that marries hard and soft power, using both in concert to address different circumstances. Smart power, he argued, must take into account not just the size of one's weapons arsenal or one's willingness to use brute force but also a deep understanding of the other party, its interests, and what constitutes an ideal outcome. It also requires understanding the context of a conflict and using that context to determine which actions to take, which tools to deploy, and how and when to deploy them.

This strikes me as exactly right, even on an interpersonal level. It is not that being controlling is stronger and being deferential is weaker. Each of these approaches can be powerful. To act with power, we each need a full arsenal, a command of both "weapons," and we need to be able to analyze the situations we are facing with an eye toward what is most likely to work, not just in terms of how strong or weak they make us look and feel, but in terms of the outcomes outside of ourselves that almost always matter much more.

Power is the ability to control others for our own purposes—that is one way to think about it. But power is also the ability to make a positive difference in someone else's life. To use power well, we often need to do both.

Who Gets to Have Power?

Myth: Power comes with status or authority.
Truth: We all have more power than we realize.

We tend to see power in others, more than in ourselves. But power exists in every relationship, not just in the lives of the rich and famous. Relationships are about people depending on one another, by definition. So no matter how small, insignificant, or powerless you feel, and no matter what role you are playing, other people need you, in one capacity or another. Take the relationship between parents and their children as an example. Intuitively, it seems obvious that parents "outrank" their children. Parents have more authority—that is, the right to tell their kids what to do. But most parents also want their kids to love and respect them, and to validate their competence as parents. This is how we parents end up wrapped around our children's tiny fingers. Using power well as a parent, in other words, depends much less on authority per se than on how well we can show our children that their needs and insecurities matter more than our own while trying to wield authority. The same is true for any other context or relationship where power differences matter.

We all have power at work as well, regardless of seniority, formal title, or position, even if it doesn't always feel that way. Of course, our bosses have more power than we do, in some ways. They control our pay, promotions, and job assignments, for example. They can hire and fire us, even make or break our careers.

Yet subordinates have power too, to the extent that they are valuable. If a subordinate is hardworking, competent, and committed, the boss, generally speaking, wants to keep that subordinate happy. This is also contextual: in an economy where labor is scarce and employees can easily leave one job and find better work elsewhere, for example, the boss has some power, but an indispensable employee could, theoretically, have more. A valued employee with rare expertise and strong alternatives has leverage; she can get more of what she wants. To have power in a particular relationship, it helps to be needed; we have to make ourselves useful to others.

Why Gender Differences Matter, but Not in the Way That You Think

Myth: Men and women approach power differently.
Truth: There are only a few small differences in how men and women approach power, but they have big effects.

It is widely assumed that when it comes to power, men and women differ in every imaginable way. It is generally true that men still have more power than women in society. But this does not mean that men care more about power than women. In fact, according to a program of research conducted by psychologist David Winter, the need for power, or what is sometimes called the power motive, is no greater in men than in women. While there are studies showing that women *report* being less interested in power than men, this is a different phenomenon. In our culture, gender roles dictate that men are supposed to care more about power than women. So when men act as though they are interested in power, they appear to be doing what they are supposed to do. Women who behave as though they are interested in power tend to be judged negatively and viewed with suspicion. So women are often reluctant to show they are interested in power, while men who are not all that interested in power are reluctant to report that other things are more important to them. Both men and women care about having power. But their interest is expressed in different ways.

For example, men tend to endorse hierarchical differences more; they believe that some groups should have more power than other groups in society, whereas women tend to endorse more egalitarian beliefs about groups and society. One way to understand these gender differences is that women are more interested in keeping others from having power over them than they are in elevating themselves over others. Consistent with these beliefs, women leaders tend to use power in slightly more democratic ways than men do; men tend to be slightly more authoritative as leaders. This difference is statistically reliable; however, the difference, on average, is not nearly as great as we tend to believe. Men are more physically aggressive than women, but women have other ways of being dominant and controlling. In short, both men and women in leadership roles do, and should, use a mix of authoritative and participative styles.

Because we see more men than women in visible high-power roles, you might think that men are more effective with power than women. And this too is a myth. It is true that men are often preferred over women when choosing whom to hire or promote. Yet once in the role, studies show that women are often perceived as more effective than their male counterparts. If you look at 360-degree performance evaluations in a wide variety of industries, women are only rarely perceived as less effective than men in high-power positions, and women often receive higher effectiveness ratings in leadership roles than men do. One large meta-analysis showed, in fact, that effectiveness ratings were higher for female leaders in almost every context, with two exceptions: male leaders received higher performance ratings in male-dominated industries such as finance and the military (where, presumably, more aggressive or authoritarian approaches to using power are more normative and valued), and, as many women might surmise, male leaders received higher self-ratings than women.

What Power Is Actually For

Myth: More power leads to more success, and more satisfaction.
Truth: It's not how much power you have but how you use it that counts.

In our culture of individualism, we tend to think of power as a tool for our own self-enhancement and a resource for our personal consumption. But if we zoom out a little, and hover above it for a moment, we can see that power differences arise in social groups like families, organizations, and communities to help solve group problems, not just individual ones. In humans and other animals, the alpha has power because of the risks he or she must be willing to take to protect the rest of the pack. Lower-ranking group members serve higher-ranking members in exchange for the right to belong, to be protected, and to be cared for with resources that others have obtained.

It is natural, and even healthy, to care about ourselves, and to ask the question "What's in it for me?" But when it comes to having or wielding power, this is not the right place to start. We seek power to the extent that we feel powerless. But actually having power, no matter how much, does little to alleviate powerless feelings. The sense of powerlessness that pervades our lives is not about power per se. It is an artifact of childhood, a survival instinct, and a response to the fact that we will not be here forever. In this one way, we are actually all powerless. The best we can do is to come to terms with this reality and focus on making a difference for others in the time that we have. To some extent, this shift in mindset happens naturally as we age. With wisdom, life experience, and the growing awareness of our mortality, we start to focus more on future generations and what we can do to help them thrive. We achieve things and start to wonder about meaning and purpose. We start to worry less about our own success and happiness and more about the success and happiness of future generations.

Why wait? Fortunately, we can all acquire this wisdom and maturity, at any age, by just learning how to think differently about the purpose of power in our lives, and in the world.

PART II

The Two Faces of Power

2

The Art and Science of
Playing Power Up

Zhu Rongji, who served as the fifth premier of the People's Republic of China from 1998 to 2003, held the highest post in one of the world's most powerful nations. As premier, Zhu broke with the party-first tradition for which China's government officials were known. He brought China's economy into the global arena, breaking up some of the country's state-owned enterprises and steering China's entry into the World Trade Organization. According to BBC News, "He had a reputation for getting things done."

After leaving his post, Zhu decided that China needed a business school and that he was going to build one. He chose his alma mater, Tsinghua University, as the site. Noting that the world's top business schools all had impressive advisory boards, he aimed high and—as a testament to his power—landed a large and incredibly distinguished group, including the CEOs of Walmart, Apple, Facebook, and Alibaba, as well as the sitting deans at Harvard, Wharton, Stanford, and MIT.

In 2016, Zhu hosted a board meeting at a lavish and formal summer palace outside of Beijing. Just to get in, guests had to pass through impeccably tended gardens and down high-ceilinged hall-ways to reach a long receiving line where Zhu held court at the far end, a translator at his elbow. It was impossible not to feel dwarfed by the setting. But once participants reached him, they found Zhu to be gracious, patient, and attentive, greeting and speaking briefly, one at a time, with more than forty attendees. The imposing physical surroundings called attention to Zhu's power and status. But his attentiveness to each of his guests as they met him showed respect for *their* power and status.

The meeting itself took place in an opulent ballroom that was theatrically staged for this purpose. Attendees were seated in a semicircle several rows deep, advisory board members on one side, Chinese dignitaries on the other. Once everyone had been seated, Zhu entered slowly and moved carefully toward the large, slightly elevated armchair at the front of the room. He took his time to step up, sit down, and settle in.

One at a time, attendees introduced themselves. The most powerful business leaders, university administrators, and political dignitaries in the world had one chance to make the right impression. Most had taken time away from packed schedules to come halfway around the world for this board meeting. Yet there were no haughty power moves in sight. One at a time, the attendees dutifully stated their names and institutional affiliations, as though no one knew who they were. And they poured it on: so pleased to be there, so honored and so grateful, their expressions of respect and deference spilling forth, one after another.

The atmosphere was very formal, but Zhu looked completely relaxed, as though he was enjoying the show in which he was starring. The attendee who told me this story observed, "He was so still and so grounded while this was happening that if he had closed his eyes, you would have thought he was meditating. Or taking a nap." Zhu teased gently as the meeting progressed about recent happenings at specific companies. He acknowledged his board chairs, calling them "good friends." And then he said, "I would like to welcome the new members," and singled out two: Muhtar Kent, the CEO of Coca-Cola, and Indra Nooyi, the CEO of PepsiCo, who, somewhat unusually, were there in the same room.

"Before the meeting," said Zhu slowly, giving time for translation, "I asked my staff, which do you prefer? Coke or Pepsi?" The room went very still. Zhu looked around, paused for effect, and grinned. "It turns out," he said, "some like Coke. And some like Pepsi." The audience exhaled, tittering. But Zhu was not done. "I, myself," he said, upping the ante, "I like both!" The laughs were heartier this time. He tipped his head back and joined in.

The Coke-or-Pepsi joke is a work of art. It not only defused the tension he caused by bringing business rivals to the same room, but also reassured the CEOs that they were equals in his heart and that he intended to be fair. It said, *We are friends, and we are in this together.* At the same time, it reminded them, and others, that he had the power to make or break any of them in China.

Zhu was a powerful actor, in every sense of these words. He had status, based on his reputation as the former premier of China. He had power, by virtue of his ability to control access to business opportunities in one of the largest, fastest-growing economies in the world. He had authority—it was the first meeting of his board, on his turf. And his power was enhanced by how he played his role.

Zhu played his power up in some ways; he never let anyone forget who was in charge. But he also sometimes played his power down, by showing respect and deference to those around him. He was in control. And yet he chose to connect. He used his power to draw others closer, not just push them away. To create bonds between others, not just pit them against one another. To create a sense of security, not just play off others' insecurities.

Power has two faces, no matter who you are. You can play it up, show it off, and remind others who has the upper hand. And you can play it down, minimize it, and remind others how important they are. Most of us tend to show one of these faces first, and to rely on it a little too much. To use power well, you will want to get comfortable showing both.

Playing High

One of the first things I noticed when I started working with actors is that most people, when thinking about how to "act" powerful, will spend most of their time worrying about what to say. Actors, on the other hand, have their lines given to them, which means they are able to spend more time thinking about physical action. And when it comes to using power, we can learn a lot by paying attention not just to words but also to *how* we deliver our lines.

Acting, as a profession, is an art, and playing power up onstage is a means of artistic expression. Actors learn how to play power up and play it down as a fundamental part of their professional training. Keith Johnstone, the British theater director and pioneer of improvisational theater, points to what he calls *status play* as a critical foundation of any relationship between two characters. For an actor, mastering these repertoires of behavior is necessary to believably inhabit the circumstances that come (and go) with the roles they play.

Johnstone uses the term *playing high* to describe what an actor does physically to try to win a status contest. No one does anything onstage out of habit, or what "feels like me." The choice to play high is strategic. It makes sense whenever the actor, in role, wants to claim more status, compel more deference, or attract more recognition— not from the audience, but from the other actors in the scene. When an actor plays high, it is a bid for more status and power.

Playing high, according to Johnstone, is doing things to raise oneself relative to others—by name-dropping, claiming expertise, or pulling rank; or to lower others relative to oneself—by criticizing or judging someone, disagreeing with them, mocking them, or ignoring them. It is easy to make the mistake of assuming that playing high always works as intended. But as Johnstone astutely observes, characters play high, both in the theater and in life, not because they are more powerful than others and they know it, but because regardless of reality, they are not sure they are respected or powerful enough. Playing high, according to Johnstone, does not necessarily mean landing on top—it is an expression of a need or an aspiration, and an attempt to stake out a claim. The message we send when playing high in life and onstage, according to Johnstone, is *Don't come near me, I bite.*

In the theater, as in life, playing high is a strategy that works in some situations but not others. Depending on how it's done and, most important, when it's done, it can communicate aggression, arrogance, disinterest, and hubris, or it can signal competence, dignity, composure, and even generosity. It should not be a way of showing up everywhere, regardless of what else is going on. You can do that. But it will look cartoonish.

The Call of the Wild

Johnstone's observations about how we "play high" show scientific acumen, and most of what he teaches can be scientifically validated. Displays of expansiveness, like spreading out, waving the arms, opening the mouth wide, and showing the teeth are all associated with what social scientists call *dominance behavior,* which refers to the ways animals of all kinds show that they are willing to use force if necessary to win a fight.

In Jack London's classic novel *The Call of the Wild,* Buck, a

St. Bernard–Scotch Shepherd mix, is stolen from his owner in California and sold in the Klondike as a sled dog. To survive in his new, (literally) dog-eat-dog world, Buck has to rediscover his most basic animal instincts. The landscape has changed from a civilized one in which the best way to get what he needed was to be friendly and cooperative—where it made sense to play his power down—to a competitive arena in which to get what he needs he might have to sleep with one eye open, bare his teeth, and even fight to the death.

In the wild, most animals (including humans) live in groups. To be accepted and maximize their odds of survival, they must figure out first how to stay safe, and second how to rise up in the pack. Sometimes they have to show deference, and at other times show dominance, as they jostle for position while trying to accomplish these goals.

To show dominance, an animal will square off, face its opponent directly, and make direct eye contact to show readiness to approach. When performing dominance displays, animals, much like humans, literally puff themselves up—in some species, they raise their hackles; in others, they rise up on their hind legs. They physically expand and increase the size of their physical footprint. And they bare their weapons—not just their teeth but also their claws and physical mass. Like humans, they "throw their weight around" to show how much they have.

It makes some people uncomfortable to think about this kind of posturing in humans. But we have to accept the fact that human beings size one another up in exactly these same ways, and we are sending nonverbal messages about our intentions toward others all the time, intentionally or not. When we act with power in the real, civilized world, regulating our body language is just as key to delivering a convincing performance as it is onstage or in the wild. We tend to trust others' nonverbal messages more than their verbal ones.

And nonverbal assertions of power can be more effective than verbal ones.

Of course, how we speak is also important. Speaking, itself, is a physical act. When playing high, an actor will speak slowly, deliberately, and in complete sentences that end definitively, with a drop in pitch or a sharp consonant. There is no rush, no apology for claiming time or attention, and no invitation for further discussion. When an actor plays high, the voice is usually deeper and more resonant—it comes from the diaphragm more than the throat. But using a whisper, intentionally, is also playing high—especially when conflict is escalating—as it demands more rapt attention from the listener and indicates complete self-control in the face of an emotional situation.

When an actor plays high, he holds his head straight while speaking. A young start-up founder I know who did not always carry himself like a CEO was coached to "put on your headdress" before going into important meetings, in reference to this posture. Imagine yourself with a heavy crown on your head, and notice what happens to the rest of you. You stand straighter, your shoulders drop, you move and even breathe more slowly, and your chin lifts just a bit to keep the thing from sliding off.

Playing high is taking up space, both literally and figuratively. An actor playing high does not hide or "kind of" come into the room. She "makes an entrance," striding in boldly, gracefully, with determination and focus, and sometimes also noisily, in high heels or heavy shoes. When playing high, an actor spreads out, leans back, and, as my colleague Dan Klein likes to say, "uses furniture wrong": putting feet on the desk, straddling the chair, draping an arm across the back of someone else's seat, reclining on an office settee; all of these are classic examples. Playing high is taking up space and maximizing personal comfort. It is moving through the scene smoothly, using the whole body in ways that demonstrate complete clarity of purpose and not a hint of hesitation or self-doubt.

Pulling Rank

Pulling rank is perhaps the most obvious example of how people play power up, particularly in the workplace. Pulling rank is explicitly claiming the right to control an outcome based on one's status or hierarchical position, as when your kids realize they can open a negotiation by asking why they have to obey your directives, and you say, "Because I'm your mom and I said so." The business equivalent is akin to how Amazon CEO Jeff Bezos allegedly expresses displeasure when his team fails to execute on a directive by asking whether he needs a letter from downstairs verifying that "I'm the CEO." As another example, Henry Ford reportedly advised those who questioned him to comply because "my name is on the building."

Pulling rank is reminding subordinates that you have the legitimate authority—that is, the right that comes with a role or formal title—to tell them what to do. It is a justification for asserting control that can be hard to argue against, and it can work very well. But it can also be alienating, especially when rank or some kind of formal authority is the only source of power one has.

Pulling rank can also mean using your authority to set ground rules and police them, which is critical for creating a functional climate in settings where work needs to get done. I know a CEO who collects smartphones and other devices in a box before a meeting begins, and I've heard of managers who bring Nerf guns to meetings and allow members to shoot at one another if they don't follow their own norms, and others who insist that rule violators have to pay a fine that goes into a group lunch pool. Another manager I know, when he was new, made an example of someone who arrived late to a meeting by pausing the action and asking the late participant to join him in the hallway. No one knew what exactly went on out there, but the manager came back into the meeting alone.

I know one professor who locks the doors when class begins, leaving late students standing outside, and another who insists on answering a student's phone herself if it rings during her class. "Hi!" she says cheerfully, with the caller on speaker, the intended recipient shrinking into his seat. Confused, the caller will inevitably ask, "Umm, can I please speak to Ron?" or "Who is this?" "This is Professor Aaker," she chirps, "and you called during my class. Ron's here, but he's busy right now. Would you like me to give him a message?" Needless to say, these kinds of things rarely need to happen more than once in a very blue moon.

Most people are loath to do it, but pulling rank can be generous, or an expression of caring, when done by the right person at the right time. Parents have a responsibility to keep their children safe and healthy. Professors have a responsibility to ensure that students learn. And a manager has a responsibility to her team for the productivity of a meeting she runs. And sometimes this means reminding people that as the person who is formally in charge, we have the right, and the responsibility, to tell them what to do.

Poking Fun

Humor is very hierarchical, because many jokes are put-downs or take-downs. Observe what happens on Twitter. Name-calling is a way of playing power up that is especially tricky to counter because attempting to do so indicates you can't take a joke. President Trump is a specialist in this technique; he comes up with catchy (if demeaning) nicknames for all of his political opponents and delivers them like verbal swipes. Trump's nicknames seem designed to diminish others, but note also the effect on his stature when he dishes it out but can't take it. Following a put-down with an attempt at a take-down can undercut your clout.

On the other hand, research by psychologist Dacher Keltner finds that in some contexts, teasing and even name-calling can belie respect and affection. Sometimes the fact that you have singled someone out for teasing communicates a special status; it says, *I can make fun of you, because we have a special bond.* I had a swim coach in middle school who used to call me "Nose"—he had a big one, too—as though we were in a special and exclusive club. On one hand, it kind of hurt my feelings, but on the other, I do think my teammates wished sometimes he had noticed something to tease them about.

Blowing Smoke

Backhanded compliments like these are almost always a kind of power play. That's because commenting on someone's appearance—whether positively or negatively—not only is objectifying but also assumes the right to scrutinize and pass judgment. This is why it's taboo for a subordinate to compliment a superior's appearance, but perfectly acceptable for a boss to compliment an underling's. An executive I know confided that one of his staff members used to pelt him with friendly comments about his appearance on a daily basis—things like "Have you lost weight?" or "I like your haircut"—and he couldn't understand why, as he put it, "it made the hair on the back of my neck stand up." These comments bothered him because they implied a level of scrutiny, a familiarity, and a right to pass judgment that subtly undermined his status as the boss. Presumably, we compliment others at least sometimes because we want to make them feel good about themselves, and there are good ways of doing this. As an example: "I'm so happy to see you!" And, while maintaining eye contact (no body scans allowed!), "You look great!" But a lower-ranking person is not supposed to judge a higher-ranking person, period, unless feedback is requested.

Pushing Boundaries (and Buttons)

This executive's visceral reaction to his subordinate's flattery highlights a widely accepted yet largely unspoken rule that defines hierarchical life: the higher-ranking person gets to draw the social boundaries and define the social norms. So intruding on a boundary, defying a norm, or behaving as though you have the right to do these things is a way of playing power up.

This particular social convention is somewhat subtle, easy to miss, and the source of many a faux pas. It's perfectly acceptable for a boss to ask a subordinate about her weekend, but much less so the other way around. Similarly, it is fine for the boss to invite a subordinate to lunch, but such an overture is a little presumptuous or somehow inappropriate in the opposite direction. As evidence, consider the uproarious reaction when a West Point cadet surprised General Norman Schwarzkopf—following a lecture he gave there in 1991, while the general was taking questions from the audience—by inviting him for a beer. Schwarzkopf was stumped, if mildly amused, and the audience burst into shouts and whistles. The cadet was playing his power up with the invitation, but while extending it he played his power way, way down, with great formality, inserting the word "sir" every few words. Schwarzkopf accepted.

The higher-ranking person decides how personal a professional relationship can be, and invitations flowing down the food chain are not expected to be reciprocated in kind. Most people get this: I have some very high-profile friends who joke that they never go out—although they entertain often themselves—because no one dares to invite them to do anything!

When a lower-ranking person acts too familiar with higher-ranking people, it makes everyone uncomfortable, and it can be hard to understand why. Being too familiar with higher-ranking others signals not just that you don't know your own place but also that you don't recognize anyone else's place either. Sometimes, a subordinate with high status can reciprocate these kinds of overtures—for example, tease in response to being teased—while a peer who has not earned the right to play it up with the boss earns disapproval for the exact same behavior.

Power can often lead those in high-ranking positions to take liberties with assuming familiarity and even intimacy that lower-status people would never dream of taking. Take, for example, the male boss who hugs his female subordinate thinking he is being friendly, not realizing that the woman, who feels she doesn't have the right to refuse this gesture, finds his behavior creepy. Sometimes this can really get out of hand. I once had a boss who leisurely flossed his teeth while we were meeting in his office, without apologizing or even acknowledging what he was doing. Lyndon Johnson used to conduct briefings while using the toilet. We once designed a study to document this tendency, and found that undergraduates, after writing about a time when they had power, were more likely to decide that the fan we had carefully placed in our lab (to blow with annoying velocity directly into their faces) needed to be moved, and did so, without asking for permission. Participants who wrote about a time when someone else had power over them were more likely to sit there and suffer. They were on our turf, but the first group did as they pleased to make themselves feel more at home.

Like most norms, familiarity norms have hierarchical content, and they are mostly invisible until someone violates them. When playing power up, you draw physical and social boundaries where you want them.

"You Are Not Worthy"

Attention is one of the main currencies of power. We simply allocate more attention to people who we think matter more. So the amount of attention garnered by specific individuals in a particular context is a reliable measure of how much power they have. Thus, a common way that people play power up is by refusing to acknowledge another person's presence or failing to give them undivided attention. This is also why showing up late to an appointment or checking one's phone during a meeting or in class is offensive, but more acceptable for a higher-ranking person than a lower-ranking one. These are moves that can be used strategically to send a message that your time matters most.

And they can backfire, even when used inadvertently, in the wrong context. For example, a former graduate student who is now a tenured professor and friend recently called me out for doing "the power thing" when I forgot I had met her fiancé on a previous occasion. It was insulting to her, and I felt terrible—though in my defense, I had met previous boyfriends on other occasions and did not know at the time that he was "the one." Whether it's intentional or not, when we act like we can't be bothered to acknowledge the existence of the people around us—or recall meeting them or even remember their names—what others are likely to hear is, "You are not worthy of my precious time or attention."

More often than not, when this happens, it is just the result of the need to prioritize and allocate attention in a world where demands on attention outstrip supply. So when the boss seems oblivious to an underling hovering in the doorway, it's not rude exactly—it is that he is distracted by something that feels more urgent. A new company founder recently told me that his employees, who work on an open floor, felt he didn't care about them because he used to hide out in his back office with the door closed. "What are you doing in your office?" I asked. "I'm freaking out back there," he told me, "just trying to keep the company alive and keep their paychecks coming in."

Inattention can also be used purposefully and constructively as a way to control bad behavior. Parents, for example, are advised to "not react" when their children act out, because a scolding, compared to inattention, can actually feel like positive reinforcement (the acting-out approach often continues when it is rewarded with attention). And a former student recently told me that he still jokes with his classmates about my not-so-subtle way of discouraging students who were hijacking the discussion at the expense of their classmates with random, off-topic comments by barely acknowledging what they had said. Sometimes, to keep things on track, you have to let one land in the sand.

Interrupting

It is generally considered bad behavior to interrupt someone while she is speaking, but it happens all the time. This can also happen by accident. Recently, a former student who launched and sold a successful start-up sheepishly confided that when he complained to a coach that his team wasn't speaking up enough, it was pointed out that he had a habit of interrupting them when they did speak during meetings. "I was just excited," he explains, "and my thoughts and ideas would kind of overflow." His intent wasn't to intimidate his employees into silence or imply that his ideas were more important than anyone else's, but that was how it came across.

When a leader dominates a conversation by interrupting, it can stifle voices and create a demoralizing and even psychologically unsafe space where others feel their opinions are not valued and they are punished for speaking. But in certain contexts, this same behavior can have the opposite effect. When a leader interrupts the most vocal members of a team or group in order to give the floor to quieter individuals, for example, the team benefits from the input and insights of those who might not have spoken up otherwise. This is yet another way playing power up can be helpful.

Many people ask me how to stand up for themselves when they are interrupted. I try to shift their perspective. Sticking up for ourselves is not the best way to shift the balance of power. We are all at our most powerful when we stop someone else from being interrupted—to me, this is the brass ring. Playing power up to protect our own interests usually ends up working against us in group contexts. But playing power up to protect others' interests almost always works in our favor. Whom would you rather have in your foxhole: the person who talks over everyone, the person who sticks up for himself when interrupted, or the person who will stop an interrupter from interrupting you?

The Right of Refusal

Saying yes is easy; supporting others in their efforts makes them happy. Saying no is harder and is an exercise in playing power up. Exercising the right to disagree, to veto, to redirect, or to refuse to comply with another person's wishes is the concrete manifestation of authority: the right to tell others what they can and cannot do. When wielded responsibly, the ability to say no is an essential aspect of using power well, especially in a high-power role. It is needed to keep teams focused on top priorities and to keep projects on schedule and under budget, and to prevent people from getting sidetracked or veering off course. Saying no is a problem only when a person in power shoots down suggestions, requests, or opportunities indiscriminately, for personal reasons that do not benefit the group.

I've had to learn the art of saying no as I've internalized the administrative responsibilities of my role as a professor. The role comes with very little power, a modicum of status, and a lot of responsibility: for making sure that students are staying on track to pass their courses and graduate successfully, and that the process I'm using to evaluate their progress is equitable. Initially, I didn't know what kind of challenges this role would present, but I have since found that much of what I do with my "authority" is say no to requests for special treatment. Most of the students I deal with in this role go about their business, get their work done, and play by the rules, and I never see or hear from them outside of class. But there are always a few whom I hear from, a lot, and it is often to ask for something to which they are not entitled. I've learned to say no in many "languages"—in person, by holding my head still instead of nodding while listening, and occasionally while also pursing my lips. In email, I control the pace to make sure I have ample time to consider requests and their legitimacy, which means I am not responding too quickly. It is sometimes important to let people know that their "emergency" is not an emergency for me. I've learned to use as few words as possible when responding, to avoid offering points that could be negotiated. I've learned to point out to people that what they are asking for is unfair to their classmates. There are many good ways to say no.

When Playing Power Up Is a Strong Choice

As you can see from these examples, playing power up is not the same as winning a contest. Whether playing it up is a winning approach to social interaction depends on the context: the setting, your objectives, whom you are dealing with, and, most important, how much power you actually have. In the rest of this book, the *how*s and *when*s are spelled out in fine detail. But for now, suffice it to say that playing power up (or down) is a learned behavior and some are more expert than others. Some of you may be asking yourselves, *Why would I ever want to do this?* You should want to learn how to play power up because there will be times when other people need you to behave this way in order to protect their interests. Some of you may be asking yourselves, *Why would I ever want to do anything else?* The same rule holds. When you are able to play power up, or down, to make those you care about most feel more secure, you are much more likely to be successful than when you do either of these things because they feel "natural" or "authentic."

Most people in most situations want the same thing: they want to impress other people and earn their respect without being intimidating or acting superior. And this is true regardless of your actual position within a hierarchy. Whether you are vying for roles among peers or operating from a superior or subordinate position, the repertoires of playing power up and playing it down are the tools you need to manage the balance. It's like standing on a seesaw—or what Harvard psychologist Richard Hackman called the "authority balance beam"—you have to know how to throw your weight around, or at least shift your weight from one leg to the other in response to what others are doing, just to avoid falling off.

Playing power up can seem hostile. But the thing to keep in mind is that in many group situations, playing power up is the most generous thing you can do. In all groups, we need someone to step up, provide direction, and keep things under control. Knowing that someone is prepared to keep things on track and shut down bad behavior immediately makes it possible for everyone to relax and stay focused on the task at hand.

When you are the person in charge, you have to be willing to play the part. You have to let people know, *I've got this.* No one wants to be a jerk. But to do right by those who depend on us, we all have to learn how and when to use power in a dominant way.

Playing power up in a subordinate role can also work, but it is riskier. In order to support the person above you, you will, on occasion, have to provide a reality check. Sometimes they will be wrong. Sometimes they will cross boundaries. Sometimes they will take unnecessary risks. Sometimes you have to let them know that if they can't change how they deal with you, you are going to want to leave. It is important to be aware of the power you have as a subordinate to protect yourself, to protect others, and to protect your boss from the risks that come with having power. The key is to have established trust beforehand, to have demonstrated that you know your place, and to convey that you are acting with the other parties' interests in mind.

Among peers, there is no question that playing power up can be an effective approach to gaining status and power. Research on social hierarchies of all kinds shows that dominance is one of the strongest predictors of who rises first and fastest into positions of influence. In a study by Cameron Anderson, Don Moore, and colleagues at UC Berkeley, for example, peer-group members who displayed overconfidence in their answers to a set of problems attained status more readily than those who were better calibrated. And later, even after group members learned their most respected teammates were wrong, the status of overconfident members was not damaged. Overconfidence is not as risky as we think, according to this study.

We all appreciate people who are willing to take personal risks to move the group forward.

So playing power up is one way to win a status contest, but it is not always the best way. A dominant or authoritative approach to using power is most appreciated and is preferred to more participative approaches when groups are in crisis and feel they need a stronger arm at the helm. In addition, studies show that when power-holders use dominance, control, and even aggression to benefit less powerful others or put themselves in harm's way to benefit their in-group, they are viewed as both competent and caring. These two qualities form the basis of trust judgments. So as a rule of thumb: playing power up is most likely to be an effective approach to using power when it is what the group needs.

3

The Art and Science
of Playing Power Down

The abilities to play power up and to play it down are both useful, even necessary, to be successful in a hierarchical world. But
most of us tend to rely more on one approach than the other. Some
of us seem destined to run things, while others seem destined to
play a supporting role. Some are better on offense and others on
defense. Some are naturally intimidating and others are naturally
disarming. Some of this is undoubtedly hardwired, but biology is
not the whole story. Playing power up and playing it down are
learned repertoires of behavior that become natural and familiar, or
not, because of who we are and what we have learned in our personal
lives about how to get what we need and be successful.

Sequoia Capital is one of the biggest players in the U.S. venture
capital business. According to some estimates, the combined current public market value for the firms that Sequoia has funded—
including Apple, Google, PayPal, Oracle, YouTube, Instagram, and
Yahoo!—is $1.4 trillion, or 22 percent of the Nasdaq. The company
is known worldwide for its power and prestige, and a meeting with
Sequoia is both a dream and a nightmare for an entrepreneur. On

one hand, winning Sequoia backing is a real feather in one's cap. But on the other, the prospect of having to impress a room full of Sequoia partners is intimidating enough that some company founders are hesitant to even approach them.

In the venture capital world, Sequoia partners are legendary for both razor-sharp intellect and killer instinct. Founded in 1972 by Donald T. Valentine, the firm's U.S. business is now run by Roelof Botha, the son of a South African foreign minister who is almost always, literally, the smartest person in the room. He graduated from the University of Cape Town with the highest grade point average ever recorded in his program, and he was the valedictorian of his class at the Stanford GSB. Botha is like a big bear. He is warm and physically formidable, and he laughs easily. But make no mistake; he'll tear your best argument limb from limb.

Botha's star rose quickly at Sequoia, and he was tapped to lead the company's U.S. operations in 2017. At the time, despite its worldwide prominence and reputation, the firm internally was struggling to adapt to the changing world around it. For example, there were about a dozen Sequoia investing partners at that time in the United States. And not one of them was female.

Botha knew this had to change. He explains, "The challenge in our business is that we have traditionally hired from our portfolio companies. Recruiting from the companies is easy in the sense that we are hiring from our existing network, so we have a lot of information about these people, and they know us, too. But then they have a tendency to look and think like us."

Going outside the network would take some effort, but Botha knew that diversity of perspective was critical to the firm's success and that they would benefit from more of it. In 2013, Botha attended a Goldman Sachs conference with Sequoia partner Alfred Lin. In one session he attended, Jess Lee, the young female CEO of a start-up called Polyvore, was pitching her company—a digital styling platform that was eventually bought by Yahoo!—to prospective investors. "She impressed me," says Botha, "so I approached her afterward and invited her for lunch."

Lee recalls that when Botha first introduced himself to her, she was over the moon. "Sequoia was interested in my company!" she says. "I thought they wanted to invest." So when she learned that what they wanted was to persuade her to leave her company and come work at Sequoia, she recalls, it was a big letdown. "I didn't want to be an investor at the time," she says. "The role didn't appeal to me at all."

Botha backed off, but he didn't give up. Two years later, Polyvore was sold to Yahoo! and Lee received a phone call. "This time they asked me to come by the office for a day. I went up to Sand Hill Road, met the team, joined some pitch meetings, and eventually realized I was at a job interview." They tried to make her an offer but she stopped them, out of loyalty to her team at Yahoo! It came as a surprise. Who says no to one of these jobs? Still, the partners were determined to win Lee over. But they had to come to terms with the fact that their normal approach wasn't working.

It was a long courtship, says Botha. Instead of their normal routine of fancy dinners, they spent time observing Lee and trying to figure out who she was and what she liked. "We wanted her to get that we were willing to adapt and relate to her as she is," says Botha. "We learned she was very down-to-earth. She had this old car, and she was really into cosplaying as her favorite comic book characters. So Jim [Goetz, Botha's predecessor] had this idea: 'Why don't we get dressed up as cartoon characters, and we'll make an offer at a coffee shop.' We both went around to costume shops on a weekend. I tried on a Flintstones outfit first, but figured that was the wrong message, me carrying a club, with my arms exposed, it was too macho. It

wasn't right. And then I tried on a Woody costume from *Toy Story*...
and Jim found a Buzz outfit, we were texting back and forth, and he
found us two matching bobbleheads."

These weren't just any old costumes. Two of the most important
venture capitalists working showed up to recruit a new partner
dressed as two of the goofiest, most lovable, and most loyal cartoon
characters Pixar had ever produced. And they didn't stop there. The
executives called in their head of design at Sequoia, James Buck-
house, to help them come up with a creative way to present the
offer. "Let's do a Wanted poster," he said, "cowboy style." And he
drew a perfect rendition of the character Jessie from *Toy Story 2,* who
joined the team of do-gooders and, incredibly, had the candidate's
first name (Jess). A caption at the bottom of the poster read, *Will you
join us on a new venture?*

They asked Lee to meet them at a Peet's coffee shop in Los Altos.
"She didn't see it coming," says Botha. "We tried to catch her off
guard." They got drinks, sat down at a table, and put on their bobbleheads to wait for her.

This time, Lee was more open. Things had changed at Yahoo! and
she was rethinking her options. When she entered the coffee shop,
Lee scanned the room for two venture capitalist types in the typical
high-end casual, Northern California professional attire. But when
she looked around, there was no one there who fit the bill, just two
random goofballs at a table dressed like Woody and Buzz Lightyear.
When she saw them, her first instinct was to sneak a photo with her
phone for Snapchat and caption it *WTF.* But then she looked again,
and they took off the heads and held up the sign. "I burst out laughing," she says, and went right over. "Yes, I'm in," she blurted. Only
later did she ask them what she was going to be paid.

"I was blown away," says Lee. "I realized it meant they wanted to
work with me and would accept me for who I really am, that they
would be okay with my weird hobbies, that they would be fun to

work alongside, and that it would feel like a team. A huge piece fell into place for me at that moment. I could see I was going to have real relationships with these people. And I felt very special."

Needless to say, what Botha and his colleagues did was not normal. But it was smart and it was strategic, and although it probably felt a little risky, it wasn't at all. They found a way to impress Lee without intimidating her, to let her know that they understood who she really was as a person and that they valued and respected her differences. Instead of throwing their weight around—offering more money, advertising their assets, trying to show how great they were—they took themselves down a notch (or two). Ridiculous? Maybe. Worth the risk? Absolutely. It cost them absolutely nothing, and it won them Lee's trust. They showed that they would do whatever it took to make sure that she felt comfortable joining the team. And it set an example internally for the firm: when it comes to executing on diversity goals, you do what it takes to get the job done.

Until the day of that interview, these uber-successful venture capitalists had done what they knew how to do best: they advertised their power without even trying—played it up and showed it off. It didn't take much effort; in fact, it just happened naturally. Playing power up is doing things—on purpose or unintentionally—to elevate oneself, to stand out, to assert control and command respect, to remind others how special you are instead of trying to hide it. It's an approach to using power that relies, at least in part, on coercion and intimidation, because playing power up is showing that you are a competitor who intends to win. As we saw in the last chapter, this is the style we tend to associate with powerful people. But as this story clearly shows, when it comes to using power well, playing power down can be a winning strategy.

These guys made a conscious, planful decision to play their power down. They tried to elevate their prospect, to downplay their power, and to cede the upper hand. Playing power down is not showing weakness. It is showing that we are strong and secure enough to take personal risks and put others' interests ahead of our own. When we play power down, we do things to show respect, consideration, and deference—not to command them—to stand down and disarm others' defenses. Playing power down is trying to connect, to pull others into the fold. Like playing power up, playing it down is an act, designed to make us appear less intimidating, less capable of winning a fight, and less ruthless than we might actually be. But this doesn't mean it isn't truthful. When we play power down, we are showing that we care more about standing with than standing out, and more about connecting than controlling. Playing power down is not giving up your power; it is deciding that winning this particular battle— in the case of the venture capitalists, winning over this particular hire—may require sacrificing some of the status and authority that are traditional sources of strength and comfort for people who rank highest.

It is often assumed that powerful people always play their power up because they can, and powerless people always play it down because they have to, but in fact, you can't take either of these things for granted. It's also assumed that playing power up is always a hostile attempt to intimidate or threaten, and sometimes this is the case. But playing power up can also be a way to take care of someone who needs protection. By the same token, although playing power down is often seen as an attempt to appease or abdicate responsibility, it can also be a way of showing respect, building trust, and making others feel safe.

Playing power up and playing it down are not simply the choices or styles of individual actors; they are always part of a conversation— like a dance or a fencing match—in which every act is a reaction to what came before. When two actors are both playing power up, it looks like a contest and you can feel the sparks flying. When two actors are both playing power down, it looks like a standoff, because when both people insist on deferring to the other, the action grinds to a halt. This was the basis of an old comic strip called *Alphonse and Gaston,* about two clownish characters who were obsessive in their deference to each other, saying, "After you!" "No, after you!" "No, I insist, after you!" When both parties insist the other "go first," it is hard for anyone to move forward.

For this reason alone, the capacity to play power both ways is an important social skill. And both approaches, when used mindfully in the right context at the right time, can be effective in getting others aligned around a common goal.

✳

Playing power down is no less useful than playing power up, but it serves a different purpose. If playing power up is a way of demonstrating authoritativeness, playing power down is a way of demonstrating approachability. If playing power up shows that you are willing to fight for others, playing power down shows that you are willing to take one for the team. Playing power down can feel risky; many people worry it will make them look weak. But playing power down is not necessarily giving up control, and it can also be a sign of strength. Playing power down is a way of balancing control with connection, reminding others that you are capable of putting them first and that you might need them to reciprocate. Whenever we play power down, we let others know that we are willing to sacrifice personal prominence to advance the group's interests. This gives others permission to do the same.

I am not talking here about pretending to care about others' interests when you don't. This is actually not all that easy to pull off, for one thing. What I am talking about is adopting behaviors that demonstrate caring by tipping the balance of power toward others.

This can be accomplished by lowering oneself relative to others: by apologizing, making fun of oneself, trying to disappear into the woodwork, allowing others to make decisions for you, or acting in ways that signal you aren't worthy of status and attention. But it can also be accomplished by raising others, relative to oneself: treating someone with deference and respect, listening to them, agreeing with them, or trying to anticipate their needs, explicitly or implicitly, to support them in pursuit of their agendas.

Keith Johnstone describes these behaviors as part of what it means to "play low." Johnstone emphasizes the often involuntary ways that we try to avoid provoking others. In life, we often do these things without intending to (and the same is true for playing high). But in the theater, actors actually choose to do these things in order to embody a character's reality. When playing low, an actor will choose to speak quickly but haltingly: sometimes stammering, using *er, um, you know, like,* and other fillers that convey uncertainty, tentativeness, and self-doubt. Playing low is often associated with talking less, in the sense that playing high is associated with taking more turns speaking. But when speaking, playing low is using more words, more sounds, and cramming all of them into less time than what you see with playing high. Actors playing low try to fill the silence. They use run-on sentences, to avoid giving anyone an opening in which they might be interrupted. An actor playing low will edit herself and trail off, or end with a rise in pitch—upspeak—as if her statements are questions that invite others' answers. When playing low, one's vocal pitch is higher, the tone breathier and more shrill or strained. Loud outbursts and shouting can also be a sign that an actor is playing low, somewhat surprisingly, because losing control conveys fear, frustration, and defensiveness: characteristics of people who feel they have lost the upper hand.

When playing low, an actor tends to break eye contact first, glance around the room, and look away while speaking. When being spoken to, on the other hand, the actor stares intently at the speaker to make sure he isn't missing anything.

While playing low, actors also smile more often than they do when playing high—and this is not because life is better at the bottom. Rather, they smile apologetically, to make sure no one else is ever uncomfortable. These kinds of smiles can seem forced, weak, frozen on the face. Oscar Wilde once described this kind of smile as "a badge of appeasement." The science of laughter suggests that giggling is also an act of submissiveness. Giggles, like controlled smiles, are an attempt to make sure no offense has been taken and to assure others that the giggler needn't be taken too seriously. Smiling and giggling often come with eyebrow lifting, nodding, leaning in, and looking up at someone with big eyes, creating a "baby-faced" appearance. And actors playing low tend to move the body in fleeting, jerky ways that convey uncertainty, hesitation, diffusion of energy, and lack of commitment. All of these actions convey the absence of threat.

If playing high means taking up space and trying to expand one's physical presence, playing low means trying to hide, physically back away, or shrink into the woodwork. An actor playing low moves quickly, shuffles quietly, and takes small steps (think of a geisha), as though trying to be invisible. Playing low is using the body in ways that show confusion, lack of direction, and self-doubt—almost as though apologizing simply for being there. When playing low, an actor acts to physically protect herself from physical and psychological threat, and exhibits discomfort—adjusting the clothes, touching the face and hair, and fidgeting. These are all compensatory habits that can be difficult, but are entirely possible, to control.

Whereas playing high conveys dominance by acting tough, playing low is accomplished by creating and exposing points of physical vulnerability in an attempt to appear nonthreatening. The message an actor sends when playing low, according to Johnstone, is *Please don't bite me, I'm not worth it.*

Backing Off

Although the actions associated with playing low are often displayed without awareness, they are strategic acts, as in the case of playing high. You play your power down for a reason. In most social encounters, most animals (including most of us humans) would prefer *not* to fight. This is an excellent survival instinct. So if one strategy is to bare one's teeth and attempt to intimidate a rival into backing away, an even safer response might be to smile with the teeth concealed and preemptively back down. It's a way of *rolling over* like animals do onto their backs in a position where they are physically helpless, so that there is no reason to attack.

Animal behaviorists use the terms *submission* and *appeasement* somewhat interchangeably to describe the ways animals try to indicate they do not pose a threat and are willing to back down in a contest for scarce resources. With humans, too, submission and appeasement communicate the absence of threat, the presence of vulnerability, and a willingness to put others' interests first. Again, it is not a sign that the animal has no power; it is a sign that in that moment, the animal does not intend to use the power it has. This, in a nutshell, is what it means to play power down.

When we think about what it means to be powerful, the term *low-key* is not what comes to mind. But the real power-holders of the world play their power down a lot of the time, in part because they have learned it has many benefits. People feel contemptuous of those above them in the hierarchy and may want access to the advantages they possess. A truly powerful person is often motivated to keep a low profile.

The Joke's on Me

Whereas poking fun at others can be a way of trying to raise ourselves above them, poking fun at ourselves is a way of trying, preemptively, to take ourselves down. We all make self-deprecating jokes
or comments from time to time, and some would say that women,
especially, are known for it. Amy Schumer's hilarious spoof on this
topic highlights the dynamic perfectly. "Amy, I love your hat," says
one of the women. "Are you drunk?" she responds. "I look like an
Armenian man!" "Congrats on your big promotion," says another,
prompting the reply "I'm gonna get fired in, like, two seconds."
Exaggerated? Perhaps. But the reason it's funny is that these conversations happen all the time. Self-deprecating humor is a classic
power-down move, and women in particular who have a hard time
accepting praise and compliments sometimes use it. Women (who
have lower status and power than men in many contexts) are socialized to make others feel good about themselves and, often, the easiest
way to accomplish this goal is to highlight all of our shortcomings
and make sure others know that we don't think we are better than
they are, in any way. Many women (and men) are loved specifically
for their use of self-deprecating humor; we always feel good about
ourselves when we are with them. But this sketch illustrates the problem. If everyone is constantly undercutting themselves, the conversation can't gain traction, there is no opportunity for candor, and
it's hard to get anything done. And in the end, no one actually gets
elevated.

It is okay to feel embarrassed when someone else calls attention
to an accomplishment, and it's normal to want to appear humble.
But if the goal is to make someone else feel better about themselves,
it's far better to accept a compliment than to deflect one. If you have
impressed someone, and you think they are wrong about you, what

does that imply about their judgment? Sometimes it is best to just say thank you and change the subject to something more important.

Asking for Help

Asking for help is a great way to show deference while also lifting others up. I know someone who employs this as a kind of negotiation strategy. She'll present her boss with a request, but frame it as a problem she is trying to solve; for example, "I have a job offer from another institution, and I'd really like to stay, so can you help me make it easier to say no?" This allows her boss to feel good about himself while also giving her what she wants (assuming he wants her to stay).

We are often reluctant to ask for help because we think others will feel put out, but research by my Stanford colleague Frank Flynn shows that, in general, most people like to lend a hand when they can. No one likes the idea of playing the sucker, but responding to a request for help can feel heroic; we all like knowing that we are needed and that we have the power to make a difference in someone else's life.

When a powerful person reaches out for help or admits an area of weakness, it can actually be a source of strength. As Howard Schultz, the former CEO of Starbucks who is credited with building one of the most successful brands and franchises in modern history, told reporter Adam Bryant in an interview with *The New York Times*, "I would say one of the underlying strengths of a great leader and a great C.E.O.—not all the time but when appropriate—is to demonstrate vulnerability, because that will bring people closer to you and show people the human side of you." Asking for help when in a position of power is a way of drawing others closer and inviting them to get in your corner.

Lines We Don't Cross

Another way to play power down is to allow others to define the social boundaries. Each of us operates within a bubble of personal space that defines the border between our public and private spheres. In most contexts, the size of a person's private bubble corresponds to their social rank, with higher-ranking people having a larger bubble that keeps others at a greater distance. This is one of the reasons that higher- and lower-ranking employees tend to cluster in different parts of a room. The lower your status, the farther away you sit from the big boss (or whoever is in charge) at a meeting. This shows respect for the higher-ranking person's right to personal space and to dictate who is "in" and "out." So sitting at a safe distance from the most senior person at the table is a way of signaling that we have not overestimated, or have perhaps even underestimated, how important we are.

Respecting that others have boundaries, whether physical or social, is a way of playing power down by showing awareness that others have the right to decide for themselves whether they want to be closer to you. For a person who ranks higher, allowing others the right to decide what kind of distance feels more comfortable to them is a way of elevating them and lowering yourself. It sends the message *You make the rules, and I'll follow them.*

Approval Seeking

The need for approval is a fundamental human motive; we all want others to like us and judge us positively. When we seek approval, we are playing power down. Some people do this by asking permission before taking action; others prefer the act-first-apologize-later approach. Either way, both permission-seeking and apologizing are acts of appeasement. They invite others to judge and redirect us. Apologizing is also conceding that the target of the apology is owed an explanation.

Being willing to grant someone greater control and greater rights than they are entitled to, based on rank alone, is a powerful way of playing power down. And the ability to show respect to others regardless of their rank by acknowledging that their approval matters is a great way to make hierarchical relationships work.

Going Along, Just to Get Along

Agreeing, complying, and deferring to others' wishes are all ways of showing that we are willing to let someone else's interests loom larger than our own. We are all much more likely to do this when dealing with people who outrank us, as we should. This is one of the strongest hierarchical norms there is, and going along with others' wishes can be a way of showing that we know our place.

But some take this tactic too far, saying yes because it seems easier in the moment than saying no, even when doing so serves nobody's interests. And no one earns status from being known as a *yes man*—someone who always agrees with the boss no matter how wrong or misguided she is. It is also a mistake to agree with someone when we don't mean it, or agree to do something when we have no intention of doing it. These behaviors are not examples of "acting"; they are examples of lying. When we say one thing with every intention of doing another, it erodes our integrity and undermines trust. It is a way of showing that our own interests in staying safe are more important than the other person's needs for honest input.

Many of us also defer when we shouldn't simply because we want to be liked. But leaders who constantly downplay their power and try to act like "one of the gang" (think Steve Carell's character in the sitcom *The Office*) will struggle to step back into the role of "boss" when the situation calls for it. In a 2003 *Harvard Business Review* article, David McClelland and David Burnham reported that managers who worried too much about whether others liked them were, ironically, disliked as managers, because they created chaotic and disorganized working environments. They also played favorites, bending the rules for difficult subordinates in order to stay in their good graces. Their employees saw them as fickle and unpredictable.

Last year, I was at a retreat with about a hundred new business founders who had received venture capital backing and were in the process of morphing from pals with a cool idea to executives responsible for managing hundreds of employees. For every person I met who feared they weren't respected enough, who feared being too nice and not authoritative enough, I met another who feared the control they were taking would make them seem like a jerk. What I wish for you, I tell such people, is that you are creating something at work that is so important to you that it doesn't matter if anyone likes you or not. If you really care, and you make that obvious—seizing power or giving it away because those actions make sense for the company given the challenges you face at that moment—the rest will take care of itself.

When Playing Power Down Is a Strong Choice

Many years ago, I attended a dinner party. The host was a friend. Our kids were in preschool together, and we had learned we shared interests. At the time, I was co-directing an executive education program for women leaders, and she was an accomplished executive, in between jobs, who was writing a book on dual-career couples. She was married to a Stanford alum, and had decided to host a small dinner for a handful of female GSB alumnae, a couple of faculty members she knew personally, and a few other acquaintances, to talk about women's leadership. It was a small, informal event. While perusing the crudités, I was approached by a cheerful young woman who introduced herself and said she had been told she should meet me. She was curious about my take on the nature of the challenges for women's leadership. She said she worked for Google, had a lot of questions, and asked if we could sit together. We did, and she was great company: warm and bubbly, open, eagerly absorbing what I had to offer and sharing personal insights, observations, and experiences. When the dinner was over, we said our goodbyes.

"Sorry," I asked, "what was your name?"

"Sheryl Sandberg," she answered. I liked her, so I tried to remember her name. I had no idea who she was.

Since then, as a member of LeanIn's advisory board, I've come to know her pretty well. By any measure, Sheryl is powerful; her name appears on many a list. She's famous, of course, and she is wealthy. And she has a very big and increasingly challenging job as COO at Facebook—one of the most powerful companies out there—in which she manages both the upsides and the downsides that those responsibilities entail.

But Sheryl's personal power—the power that explains all of her success to date—has less to do with any one professional role, and far more to do with how she approaches relationships. Sheryl Sandberg is extraordinarily talented, extremely hardworking, and unbelievably focused. And despite the challenges Facebook is currently facing for having been exploited by hostile actors to corrupt our elections process, I also believe she might be the most caring person I have ever met. Sheryl is warm, friendly, and disarming, and she knows that about herself. But more important, her practice is to take her commitments to others seriously. She wants to help, to make a difference, and to be useful, and this is evident in how she goes about managing her relationships—by making introductions; offering insight and advice; referring people for jobs, promotions, and boards; holding those who work for her accountable; and building communities to advance the causes she cares about.

When we talk about power and where it comes from, Sheryl is genuinely puzzled: "Does anyone think power is about dominance anymore?" Sheryl's power doesn't come from manipulation or control, or from throwing her weight around; rather, it stems from the genuine desire other people have to stay connected to her, and to reciprocate her caring behavior.

Playing power down is low-key, but it can be high impact. It's how we forge connections, establish trust, and make people feel safe in our presence. Deference may not be what comes to mind when we think of powerful action, yet even in our hypercompetitive twenty-first-century culture, showing deference is a common, viable, even highly successful way of using power that is often associated with gaining more. It seems obvious when you think about it. In order to move up in a hierarchy, you first have to show others respect. As one executive I know put it, "Deference is how you earn the right to lead."

Studies of peer groups bear this out. In one study, psychologist

Joey Cheng and her colleagues asked teams of students to complete a group decision-making exercise and, afterward, to rate one another on how influential each of them was. Each team member also received ratings from teammates and outside observers on various behaviors: controls others, listens, shares expertise, and defends one's own position. Dominance, a combination of ratings the researchers defined as "the use of force and intimidation to induce fear," predicted status and influence—as expected. But the researchers also identified an alternative approach that was equally successful. Prestige, defined as "the sharing of expertise or know-how to gain respect," was associated with students who were assertive and engaged, but instead of arguing or trying to force their views on others, they listened, were responsive, spoke more tentatively, and offered their ideas on an as-needed basis. This more deferential style of participating turned out to be just as predictive of status, power, and influence as dominance was. The difference was that, by the end of the experiment, students with high prestige ratings were liked as well as respected. They were viewed as having special abilities, making valued contributions, and being likely to succeed. Students who tried to dominate, in other words, achieved power—but in this situation, it came at a cost.

The lesson is this: in a group of peers, when you are vying for status and influence, there is more than one way to the top. You can play power up and be feared, or play power down and be loved. And either way, if your approach adds value—because you know some things and are willing to take risks to share them—you can end up in a powerful position.

Many have argued, in fact, that playing power down is a better approach to managing a team overall. Whenever the person in charge needs more information, needs buy-in for effective implementation, and is working with an experienced team, the benefits of playing power down outweigh the costs. An authoritative, dominant approach to using power, which relies on fear, is associated with better performance only when the manager knows best and can count on the full commitment of those who are tasked with execution. In addition, an autocratic approach to managing is associated with higher productivity when the boss is actually watching, but a more deferential, democratic approach to management is associated with higher productivity, creativity, learning, and commitment when the boss is not present. Management experts call this style *participative leadership,* an approach characterized by involving subordinates in the decision-making process: soliciting their knowledge and expertise (without necessarily abdicating control), paying attention to their strengths and interests, and even pulling back to let lower-ranking employees take ownership of higher-level strategies. Participative leadership is playing power down by elevating and empowering subordinates to choose a course of action, rather than trying to control outcomes and how they are achieved. And it involves lowering oneself by talking less, asking questions, and using more tentative speech. Participative leadership, in other words, relies on playing power down.

And although people tend to flock to authoritative political leaders in times of crisis, at all other times, participative leaders are actually preferred. A recent study by linguists Ari Decter-Frain and Jeremy A. Frimer, for example, found that public approval of Congress was highest when politicians "used tentative language, expressed both positive emotion and anxiety, and used human words." The researchers concluded that in this context, warmth was more important than competence when trying to predict influence. Consistent with these observations, Yale University's Victor Vroom finds that although on average most managers report relying more on authoritativeness than the alternative, more participativeness is better across contexts. Studies also find that even managers who think they are participative are not playing their power down as effectively as they could be. Subordinates see their bosses as more authoritative than bosses see themselves.

In short, although most managers worry about how to play their power up more effectively, they may benefit more from mastering the art of playing power down. It's not rocket science, but when we are worried about how much power we have, it can be hard to let go.

We all want to be taken seriously. But it is not always the most important thing. A former student who used to lead a large multinational support organization explains why. She was based in the U.S. headquarters and oversaw teams across the globe. One was based in India, where businesses tend to be more hierarchical than in the United States, and it took her some time to adjust to how deferential her Indian subordinates were to her. "I often left our meetings feeling like my team hadn't fully shared what they were thinking," she says, "and that they were trying to agree with me instead of giving their honest opinion."

She decided the most effective way to improve the dynamic was to try to bridge the distance between herself and her team. So she arranged a trip to the office in India with the goal of building these relationships. She met with each person individually, but instead of using that time to talk about work, she tried to get to know the person and help the person get to know her. Instead of having lunch at her desk, she ate lunch with the team every day. And even though she was jet-lagged from travel, she went out to dinner with them every night. "I even went out to laser tag with the team," she reports, "which really helped them view me as less of an authority figure because I am terrible at laser tag."

It worked. By intentionally playing her power down, she recalls, "I was able to interact with the team in a way that made them feel comfortable being direct with me about what was and wasn't working. It allowed us to operate more effectively."

Smart Power

Most of the time, you will do what comes naturally and it will work well. You have been doing these things your whole life. But you can also become more conscious and purposeful and think of how best to play your role when what comes naturally isn't working, or when facing a challenge that is new.

I'm often asked how to make a good first impression when roles are ambiguous. A good rule of thumb, especially in a new situation, is to notice where your partner is starting, and to play power up enough to be taken seriously, while playing it down as needed to avoid posing a threat. The key thing to remember in those moments is this: power—at least the kind that lasts—comes from doing what is best for the group, in terms of advancing shared goals and interests, even when that feels risky and "inauthentic." Sometimes this requires stepping up and taking charge even when we aren't sure we have the standing. Other times, this requires stepping back and letting someone else be in charge.

You may not get it right every time. What matters is that you try. When you do, your superiors will feel supported. Your subordinates will feel protected. Your peers will find you easy to deal with. Your actions will make others' lives easier. And you will gain status for that.

To act with power, and do it well, you have to own the power you have so that you can use it with conscious intent, instead of relying on the instinct to protect yourself. Fortunately, studies show that this orientation toward power is, and can be, learned.

PART III

Taking the Stage

4

Getting in Character

How to Be Yourself Without Losing the Plot

When I first started bringing professional actors and directors into the MBA classroom, the level of interest among students just barely outstripped their skepticism. Intellectually, they could see the potential of studying acting as a way of learning to use power, but they were not comfortable with the idea of "acting" in real life. In the abstract it felt manipulative and fake. They didn't want to "be" somebody else. They wanted to be themselves, only better.

At the start of each class, I would watch them file in and "be themselves." "Hey! How's it going?" one would ask. "Great!" came the unvarying response. "How was break? How was the party? How is the job hunt?" "Awesome!" was always the answer. They had swagger. They were always smiling. You would have thought their lives were idyllic. But I knew better. They would take those masks off in my office. They were dealing with health challenges, family tragedies, visa issues, and relationship problems, and some were struggling academically to the point that they were on the verge of flunking out. These were the same people who were doing "great!"

and "awesome!" when I saw them in class, and no one was lying exactly. They were acting. They were making choices about which sides
of themselves to reveal, and which to keep behind the curtain.

This kind of behavior is normal, helpful even, in a number of
ways. In his well-known book *The Presentation of Self in Everyday Life*,
Erving Goffman described how "being oneself" is, essentially, a performance. We are all motivated to show ourselves in the best possible light, he argued, and to do this takes effort and planning. We
strategically choose costumes and props, manners of speaking and
moving, and even which stages to appear on, not to trick people into
believing falsehoods about us but to define ourselves and express a
stable, coherent identity that keeps us grounded psychologically as
we grapple with the messiness, self-doubt, and confusion that are an
inevitable part of the internal experience. Social interactions, according to Goffman, are performances. "Being oneself," in other
words, is an act.

Acting, then, is not trying to be someone else. Acting is a disciplined approach—a code of conduct—for managing yourself. That
probably sounds oxymoronic. But actors are simply people who, like
the rest of us, must manage the noisiest parts of themselves—their
feelings, their needs and insecurities, their desires, their habits, their
performance anxieties, and their fears—in order to bring the more
useful parts out at the right moments. And really, isn't that what we
all want to do? Bring out the best parts of ourselves, instead of
checking out, hiding out, or opting out by failing to show up at all?

In our individualist culture, where personal agency is a sacred
value, we tend to define ourselves in terms of personality—that
unique collection of traits that explains all of our actions and is supposedly constant across contexts. Whether we think of ourselves as
shy or outgoing, high-strung or laid-back, agreeable or argumentative, or anything else, we tend to believe we should always be who we

really "are," and do what we always do, regardless of the situation. We don't like the idea that we might change how we act or how we present ourselves in response to others' expectations. But we do this, all the time, already. And sometimes, even most times, we should.

The Art of Being Yourself

In life, as in the theater, we all have roles to play, and some roles come with more power than others. Different roles come with different scripts, or what psychologists call *schemas,* that prescribe in broad terms how we are supposed to behave. At home, the parent is supposed to protect the child, to make choices for the child, and to boss the child around if necessary, whereas the child is expected to do as the adults say. In the classroom, the professor is supposed to speak with authority about what is true and correct and assert the validity of his knowledge and experiences when appropriate over the knowledge and experiences of the students. Students are supposed to listen, request permission to speak, and turn in assignments on time, whether they feel like doing those things or not. At work, the person running the meeting is supposed to keep things on track, define what is and what is not on the agenda, and control how others participate, whereas everyone else is supposed to show up, wait for direction, and follow along.

I am not suggesting you should "fake it until you make it" or try to be someone you are not. I am suggesting that you try to accept the reality of the stage you are on: to immerse yourself fully in it, commit to being there, and show up as a version of yourself that makes sense. It is not enough to be yourself, to trust your instincts, or to do what comes naturally, out of habit. Instead, we need to pause, look around, and put ourselves in the right frame of mind—or step into the right shoes, as one of my students puts it—to do what we need to do to play our respective parts. The goal is not just to shine as ourselves. The goal is to make others look good too. And to do that, we have to stick to the plot.

Sticking to the Plot

Serena Williams delivered an unexpected performance during the 2018 U.S. Open finals, on the biggest stage in professional tennis. Normally so composed and in control on the court, Williams has shown herself time and again to be more than capable of good sportsmanship and rising above her emotions. But on that day, for a few moments on center court, she lost it. She was struggling to keep up with Naomi Osaka, a relative unknown, who had idolized Williams most of her life. As the match got more and more heated, the chair umpire handed Williams the first of two penalties, and she began to unravel. At first, she was reserved, quietly challenging his call that she had cheated by receiving coaching from the stands. But she played her power up, schooling him about his lack of experience with her as a player. When he didn't back down, she smashed her racket and received a second penalty. Instead of backing off, she approached him again, saying he owed her an apology. Instead, he gave her a third penalty for "verbal abuse." She lost a game, she lost the match, and she lost $17,000 for the three code violations. After the match, while still on camera, she appealed to the referee and claimed her treatment was sexist, which, to be fair, was debated by experts for days afterward. But her actions on the court that day were not helpful to her, or her opponent, who, having beat Williams fair and square, was robbed of her moment in the spotlight.

Serena Williams had every right to feel her anger and to wonder whether she was being treated fairly. But her timing was off. Serena Williams is a champion and a powerhouse in every sense of the word. And at the U.S. Open, no matter how famous or accomplished you are as a player, the umpire is the boss.

The British have an expression for this kind of thing; they call it *losing the plot.* Losing the plot, like "going rogue," describes acting in a way that is inappropriate because it does not fit the context and violates social norms in a way that is not helpful to anyone. In life, as in the theater, the plot is the premise; it refers to the story line, the part of the given circumstances that defines what the actors have agreed to come together to do, and how they have agreed to behave while doing it. Losing the plot is like showing up to play your part in one story and, midperformance, losing track of where you are, why you are there, and what you are supposed to be doing. It would be like Darth Vader bursting into song on the bridge of the Death Star.

To use power well, we need to stick to the plot. We need to accept that in all but the most private of moments, we are there to play a role in a story that is not just our own. This means staying connected to shared realities about who does what, when, and how, and it means following the rules of decorum and etiquette, because these are the ways we show one another we care about their outcomes too. The ability to stick to the plot—to get in character, follow the script, and behave in a way that advances shared objectives—in large part defines what it means to be an effective social actor, not just onstage but in our everyday lives.

When we act as though we have more power than we actually have, or downplay our power in ways that don't make sense to the people around us, we have lost the plot. This happens to all of us from time to time, when our own drama overwhelms us. Sometimes the consequences are trivial—like if the boss asks "How was your weekend?" and you accidentally share too much personal information. In my first semester of graduate school, I wished a very famous professor "Good luck!" before his annual seminar presentation to the students and instantly knew I had said something wrong. He did not need the encouraging words of some new graduate student to be successful that day. I had gone off-script, lost track of the realities of the situation, and said something that might have seemed inappropriate. Instead, "I'm looking forward to your seminar today" would have conveyed more respect for his position. But I was distracted by my own insecurity in his presence and ended up projecting my feelings onto him.

Sometimes, losing the plot has serious, even criminal, consequences. Whenever we lose track of our roles and responsibilities because we are too focused on ourselves, our fears and insecurities, we risk doing lasting damage to our reputations and relationships. To play our current roles well—and, more important, to step confidently into new ones—we need to let go of old habits. We need to put our inner children to bed. We need to stretch beyond outdated ways of seeing ourselves and ways of relating to other people. The ways we all act out our fears may feel authentic, but they are not always helpful. Everyone has a history with power that gets carried into adult roles in one form or another. When stepping into new roles that don't fit with the old way of doing things, we have to make adjustments. To use power well, it's not enough to be able to do the things that have worked elsewhere, or to play our parts in ways that feel natural and safe. We have to get comfortable doing the new things that feel unnatural but make sense on the stages where we are standing. It is not a question of being yourself or trying to be someone else. It is a challenge of aligning your thoughts, feelings, and actions with your responsibilities to other people.

Role-Taking and Responsibilities

In the abstract, we think of power in terms of rights and privileges. But on the ground, when power comes with the roles we are actually playing, it tends to activate responsibilities. Research shows that people who define themselves more in terms of roles (e.g., spouse, child, manager) than attributes (e.g., intelligent, fun-loving, introverted) are more likely to put responsibilities ahead of needs, and this is also true in studies of power. Political psychologist David Winter found that U.S. presidents who were firstborn children had careers that were less marked by scandal—they were less likely to have engaged in marital infidelity or sexual misconduct or to have struggled with addictions—than those who were last-born or only children. This result is consistent with studies showing that birth order predicts feelings of responsibility and the ability to delay gratification in childhood.

This is because being the "big brother" or "big sister" generally involves making personal sacrifices and looking out for younger siblings' well-being in ways that being the "little brother" or "little sister" does not. Older siblings do not play "the baby" for long; the role is usurped by the new, needier baby, and they are forced earlier into the more "grown-up" position of needing to master control of their selfish impulses and put others' needs first. Firstborn children, psychologists reason, learn from an early age that they can't always have what they want when they want it because there are others in the family whose needs are no less important. People who are rewarded for putting others first learn to do it willingly and to see that as an end in itself. And they carry this mindset into adult roles where it affects how they use power.

Studies have found similar effects for women in power, as opposed to men, for the same reason. Girls and women are socialized to see themselves as nurturers and to play the role of caretaker in most cultures. So we should not be surprised that many studies find that women—on average—use power more responsibly and are less prone to corruption than men. Data from the microfinance world support this conclusion as well. Muhammad Yunus, the Bangladeshi founder of Grameen Bank, an organization that provides microloans to individuals and small businesses in impoverished regions, has found that women tend to use these loans more responsibly than men: to buy a chicken or a goat or some seeds, which generate additional resources to feed malnourished children or to send them to school. Yunus also found that women were more likely to repay the loans than men were.

This does not have to be about gender. It is a question of how people of all genders define themselves: as individual agents versus members of a community, as lone actors versus part of a cast or a production. People who see themselves as part of a group define self-interest in terms, at least in part, of what is in the interests of the people they feel most connected to. And this makes them more responsible with power.

This means that social hierarchies in which some people have more power than others can be a constructive force in social and organizational life, but only when all of the players completely buy in. When we think of achieving power as an accomplishment without internalizing what our own power means for other people, or when we pretend that roles and the power differences among them don't matter, we fail to do right by the people who depend on us. We create a culture of insecurity. Trust breaks down. When we don't really commit to playing our roles, others don't know how to play theirs. No one looks out for anyone else, and no one knows how to behave. Hierarchy works when subordinates commit to play the subordinate role, regardless of their feelings about whether they are entitled to a better part, and when superiors commit to play the "lead" role, regardless of their insecurities or whether they feel "ready." A role, once it has been assigned, is not a personal choice. How you play it, on the other hand, is deeply personal.

When my students flashed big smiles and claimed that life was "awesome" when meeting in the classroom, they were acting, in part, with self-image in mind. But they were also showing up as the version of themselves they thought would be most helpful to the rest of us. They knew that playing the role of the happy, high-potential but not-too-full-of-oneself MBA student—which every one of them was, in addition to other things—was what was expected of them in that context. Students show up in class to learn. If everyone—including me—came into the classroom with all of their personal baggage on display, it would be impossible for anyone else to get what they came for. Making choices about which sides of oneself to show and which to hide is generous, and necessary to maintaining the social order. Acting, by this definition, is an approach to managing yourself that puts responsibility to others first in order to create a secure environment in which everyone else can do the same.

Jockeying for roles. Roles are not always assigned, of course; sometimes we have to fight for them. And power plays a part here too. Even and perhaps especially in more informal contexts where there are no official titles or reporting relationships, people try to claim roles that they think bring status and security. Or at least, I've noticed, they try to claim roles that will keep them off the bottom of the pecking order, where they are at risk of not belonging at all. Without the clarity of a formal hierarchy, we have to figure out on the fly where we fit in and how to stand out.

This is true in families, for example, where it is unusual to see siblings playing the same role. Instead, they try to differentiate themselves, to claim special status as "the athletic one," "the funny one," "the smart one," or, if necessary, "the needy one." We all seek unique roles in which we can make unique contributions and add unique value; this helps to ensure we have a special place in the group, and that our needs for belonging and acceptance are met.

Getting in character without the help of formal titles and reporting relationships is not only about understanding who has more power, but also about the reasons you have the power you do have in the first place: Is it your expertise, your social connections, or the fact that you are the most intimidating—or least intimidating—person in the room? A female general counsel I know once complained that although her legal advice was rarely questioned on the executive team, her business advice was not taken as seriously (despite her extensive experience). She wondered whether being female played a role. I reminded her that because she was a lawyer, and it was her job to play the role of traffic cop—to tell her colleagues to slow down and follow the rules of the road—they probably viewed her as a conservative influence (the lawyer in the room), which might have made her business input suspect. Realizing that her role on the team was to offer unwelcome advice changed how she played it. She said it was liberating to realize that she was an outsider because her role required it. It made it easier for her to speak louder and push harder and not to feel offended when they told her to stay in her lane. We can't always control how others perceive us or the roles we play in their personal dramas. But we can always control how we react to what comes our way.

I was always impressed by the example of John Clendenin of Xerox, who had interned at the company while in business school and was brought in after graduating to manage a man with twenty years of experience—and to whom he had reported as an intern. Clendenin came in with new formal power, but his former boss, Tom Gunning, had more status and experience in the firm. No doubt, this was awkward. But Clendenin faced it head-on. He found out where Gunning's favorite restaurant was and took him out to lunch for a frank discussion. "I did not put you in this situation," he said, but added, "you can make this a win-win." Clendenin knew he needed an industry veteran with deep contacts and knowledge of the organization by his side in order to be successful, and he told him so: "I need you. . . . I am a loyal person and will stand by you. . . . But you have to help me. If you are not going to make this work, then stay out of the way." Clendenin let his subordinate know that he was willing to play his power up, if necessary, to play his role effectively, but that he also stood ready to take care of his subordinate if he could count on him to do the same. Gunning reported that Clendenin's candor worked and the two became close colleagues.

To use power well, we need to take our roles seriously, to see ourselves as part of something greater: as someone for whom self-interest includes advancing causes greater than oneself, not just as a means to an end but because doing right by other people is an end in itself. In fact, this is what roles are for, to advance group causes. And when we take our roles seriously, this in turn makes us stronger. As columnist David Brooks once wrote: "We are all fragile when we don't know what our purpose is, when we haven't thrown ourselves with abandon into a social role, when we haven't committed ourselves to certain people, when we feel like a swimmer in an ocean with no edge. . . . People are really tough only after they have taken a leap of faith for some truth or mission or love."

Embracing the Role

Often we decide (unconsciously) which roles to take seriously based on our internal drama, rather than the shared plotlines, and it becomes harder to use power effectively. I learned this lesson the hard way from an assistant who needed more from me. She was smart and hardworking, like most assistants I've had. And she was extremely respectful when we first met, maybe more than usual. It was her way, I think, of telling me what she needed from me: to take charge. But I didn't get it. I wanted her to like me, to feel comfortable around me, and I didn't feel I had the right to make demands. So I was friendly but too "hands-off." I wasn't attentive or engaged enough; and on occasion, I dropped the ball. I was playing my power down—way down, in retrospect—because it was how I felt most like myself and it was a strategy that had worked for me in the past. But she could see that I was not taking my role seriously, and she began to get annoyed, understandably, and a little passive-aggressive. If I wasn't committed to playing my role as the caring and responsible boss, she wasn't going to commit to her role as the respectful subordinate.

I could see the relationship fraying but didn't understand why. I'd taken this approach in other relationships, but some tolerated the power vacuum around me better than she did. This gal needed more structure. Someone had to take the reins, and if I wouldn't do it, she had to try.

As is often the case with these things, the solution came to me as soon as I stopped thinking about it. In this case, it came to me while I was sleeping. Decades earlier, while I was in college, I had worked for a guy named Mike, a retired Marine who managed the fitness facilities at a large resort in the Catskill Mountains. Mike was a character. He was broad-shouldered and dressed all in white every day, and he strutted around the place like he was the master and commander—chest open, chin lifted, with perfectly feathered hair. Mike ran a very tight ship. During my job interview, after asking me a series of rapid-fire questions, he picked up a piece of lead pipe, tossed it into the deep end of the pool, and pointed. "Go get it," he said. I did.

I got the job. In May, freshman year ended, and I reported for duty, along with five other college students hoping for extra cash and a fun summer experience. Our first assignment was to scrub the toilets. Mike led us to the public restrooms and pointed. Some people quit on the spot, but I held my nose, literally, and picked up a brush. In June, when the guests started arriving, those of us who had not defected were each responsible for an area of the pool deck that contained about a hundred lounge chairs, a hundred thick mattresses, and ten heavy umbrellas, which we set up and serviced each day, then broke down, straightened out, and made spotless every night. It was hard work. And each evening, when we thought we were finished, Mike would come check our areas before letting us leave. He would get down on his stomach, lie flat out on the cement pool deck in his white uniform, and turn his cheek to the stone, eagle eyes peeled for any stray items of trash under the chairs. If he spotted something, he'd bark out the chair number. Or he would walk over and point at it.

I had not thought of Mike for years, but out of the blue one night he crept into a dream. He was pointing at a deck chair. There was nothing under it, but there was someone on top of it—a young woman in shades, stretched out like a boss. It was my assistant.

When I woke up I was amused, but then it hit me: something was wrong with this picture. In the dream, I was the pool girl, and my assistant was "the customer." My subconscious had conjured Mike to teach me a lesson: I had a mess to clean up.

But how? I thought about how Mike would handle it. And I saw him pointing.

Shortly thereafter, I received an email that I didn't like from my assistant. The tone was disrespectful. I asked her to come to my office at a specific time. I printed a copy of her email message and highlighted the offensive sentence. She knocked at my open door. I stood and, with an open hand, motioned for her to take a seat. I placed the printout in front of her, and then, channeling Mike, I pointed: "What did you mean by that?" I removed my hand from the page, looked her straight in the eye, and watched the blood drain from her face. She began to speak quickly, apologizing in every conceivable way, trying to explain herself. I watched her in silence until she was done. And then I let a few extra seconds pass. "Okay," I said. "Thanks for coming in."

It was unlike any interaction we'd ever had before, or have had since. I played my power up, and she played hers down; that is to say, each of us had gone to exactly where we needed to be. The change was immediately palpable. From then on, each of us was a little more careful, and a little more committed to playing our roles. And while we never discussed what happened, our relationship just started working. It still works to this day.

It was a huge moment in my development. Acting the way I did in that meeting felt artificial in some ways—it was staged, and none of it felt natural or "normal" to me. But I knew that if I wanted to do right by this subordinate—and the many to come after her—I was going to need a way to worry less about being myself and act like the person in charge.

Acting is purposeful self-expression, and to give a meaningful performance requires that we commit to our roles. But actors in a play know how the story ends—whether their character succeeds or fails, and why—whereas in life, of course, we don't know how anything ends; we are making it all up as we go. We don't always have time to rehearse, or a director to tell us the "right" way to play it. In life, we spend most of our time just winging it. This uncertainty can be terrifying, so it's always tempting to cling to what feels familiar. But to succeed in the world, as onstage, you have to be willing to step outside your comfort zone.

Like actors, we need to use more of ourselves—more heart, more guts, more clarity of purpose, and, importantly, more imagination— to play our roles effectively. Sometimes we need to use less of ourselves too—less fear, less shame, less "should." Instead of wasting energy trying to hide the parts of ourselves we fear the most, or trying to appear "normal," acting demands owning all of it, digging deeper, and having the courage to bring even the scariest parts to life.

The challenge of getting in role can seem daunting if you don't know where to begin. Professional actors, of course, use what is known as "technique." They understand that they're not actually the characters they're playing. Just like the rest of us, actors have to find a way to close the gap between how they approach the world in their nonprofessional lives and how the characters they are playing approach the world. To create the most natural, truthful performances, actors strive to internalize a character's circumstances and make them their own.

The Unbroken Line

Konstantin Stanislavski is most widely known as the acting teacher responsible for this approach, or what is now broadly referred to as "method acting." But Stanislavski was also an actor, a director, and owner of the prestigious Moscow Art Theater. An avid lover of the circus, ballet, and puppetry, Stanislavski honed his craft by going out into the world "in character." He would disguise himself as a fortune-teller or a tramp and wander about the city to experience what life was like in someone else's shoes. By doing so, he believed, he could play these characters more truthfully onstage.

Though it dates back to the early twentieth century, the Stanislavski method continues to provide a core foundation for the craft of acting as it is practiced today. Instead of merely acting out scenes exactly as rehearsed, or posing as a character onstage, Stanislavski proposed the actor should aspire to experience or live the role as the action was unfolding. He believed that an actor should strive for what he called an "unbroken line" of experience while performing. It was not that the actor should try to become the character she was playing, per se. Rather, the actor should imagine in as much detail as possible what it might be like to personally experience that character's reality. The unbroken line is like a seam that binds the actor and role together. Sanford Meisner, another legendary acting teacher who built on Stanislavski's work, put it this way: "Acting is living truthfully under the given imaginary circumstances." We can all approach our roles this way, like artists, by bringing personal interpretation to the performance of what is given.

The Magic If

To live truthfully in unfamiliar circumstances, many actors use variations of Stanislavski's method, by trying to imagine and internalize the character's circumstances "as if" they were their own.

A few years ago, I had the occasion to try this technique. I was a key witness for the defense in a lawsuit. I was going to be deposed. I knew that the prosecutor's intent and his only hope was to try to attack my credibility. He was going to ask me embarrassing personal questions and try to make it seem as though I had something to hide.

I felt extremely vulnerable. I knew the defense was counting on me to show up and look credible, to answer questions truthfully, and to choose my words carefully. At the same time, I was facing a hostile lawyer with a lot of experience. And I was facing him on his turf. I knew I was going to have to protect my personal boundaries and find some way to remain calm and clearheaded while being attacked. I was not going to let that prosecutor define my character on that stage that day. I needed a strong alternative to internalize ahead of time.

Then, the night before the deposition, I watched *Game of Thrones*. I'm not a regular fan and, truth be told, the show had not really captured my attention before. But that night when flipping the channels I became transfixed by the story line of Daenerys Targaryen, the fair, petite queen who as a child had been sold by her brother into sexual slavery and was now emerging as one of the show's most powerful rulers (I believe this was in Season 5). Daenerys aspires to be righteous but also feared. Having found, cared for, and hatched a triad of dragon eggs, she was now mother to three enormous fire-breathing dragons who had become, basically, her bodyguards. She was powerful despite feeling vulnerable; a protector of dragons and also in need of their protection. The Mother of Dragons. Her character spoke to me.

The next morning, as I was suiting up to be deposed, she popped into my head. I looked in the mirror and envisioned her striding toward me across a barren landscape wearing that cape with epaulets that stuck out like little wings. I swapped my black sweater for a blue blazer with real shoulders built in and instantly felt more like someone who knew what she stood for and had little to fear. What if I too was the Mother of Dragons, I wondered. What else might I do?

And the more I thought about it, the more real it became. If I was the Mother of Dragons, that meant I had children, which I do, so I knew what that was like. I felt them near me in my heart and in my body, the way a mother does, even though I couldn't see them. The dragons were too big to fit in my daughters' bedrooms, obviously, so I imagined them lounging like cats in a patch of sun on my driveway, waiting for me to come out of the house and tell them where we were going. As I drove to the office of the opposing counsel, they flew close behind, providing air cover while flanking my car. I entered the courtroom, and they followed, the sounds of their big claws clacking on the floor with my heels. They settled behind my chair.

I locked eyes with the deposing attorney. "Bring it on, sucker," I said to myself. "They breathe fire."

It might sound wacky, but this stuff is no joke. Stanislavski believed that by fully engaging the senses to imagine all the sights, sounds, tactile sensations, and smells that might be part of a character's experience, an actor could disarm the defensive impulses that normally drive our behavior and compel us to cling to the vulnerable selves we think need protection. For this reason, Harvard psychiatrist Bessel van der Kolk (known for his pioneering work on post-traumatic stress disorder) recommends drama as therapy for patients whose defenses have overtaken their lives. When the need to protect ourselves evaporates, we become capable of more. We can turn ourselves over completely to a new set of circumstances. This is how an actor brings a character to life, and it is an effective tool for acting with power, no matter what you do for a living, when "being yourself" is not working.

The Magic If is an exercise in using your imagination. It can't change the reality of who you actually are or the reality of your actual circumstances, but it can change how you experience yourself and your circumstances. These interpretations of our own life circumstances matter; they profoundly affect our outcomes. Research on self-fulfilling prophecies and stereotype threat, for example, shows without a doubt that the things we fear may be true tend to come true. Why not use the Magic If to create a reality for yourself that is based not on how powerless you fear you are but on how powerful you might be?

When facing a challenge that makes us feel powerless—a new role, a tough conversation, an unfamiliar situation—it helps to ask ourselves, ahead of time, not *Who do I fear I might be in there*, but *Who do I hope I might be like in there? What character can I internalize to have the impact I aspire to?* It might be the courage and fortitude of General Patton; the nerdy compassion of Mr. Rogers; the playful, quick-footed self-assuredness of soccer star Tobin Heath; the laid-back cool of Barack Obama; the cheerful optimism of Ronald Reagan; the mischievous kindness of Ellen DeGeneres; the fierceness of Beyoncé; the polite doggedness of Anderson Cooper; the matter-of-fact mastermindedness of Jeff Bezos; even the "wise, no-nonsense, unconditional positive regard of my grandmother"—all of these are characters my students have channeled to help them bring more of what they needed into specific performances.

Oprah's Ten Thousand

A few years ago, Oprah Winfrey was a guest on campus at Stanford and was interviewed in our "View from the Top" speaker series. In front of a packed house in a six-hundred-seat venue, a student stood up and asked her how she handles going into an important meeting where she knows she will be the only woman or person of color there. Without skipping a beat, Winfrey replied that she does not go in alone. "I come as one," she said, but "I stand as ten thousand," drawing inspiration from the Maya Angelou poem "Our Grandmothers," which is a tribute to the poet's ancestors and the battles they fought for her freedom. Angelou wrote, "No one, no, nor no one million / ones dare deny me God. I go forth / alone, and stand as ten thousand."

When Winfrey walks into an all-white, all-male boardroom, she makes a choice about how to play her part. She takes a moment and calls up a spiritual army. Winfrey doesn't make her entrance as the only woman of color in the room. She enters the room with her people in her mind and in her heart, in her experience, as one of many women of color who have played big roles and bit roles elsewhere, at other times in history.

In her NAACP Hall of Fame Award acceptance speech, Winfrey

made reference to this way of thinking about the role she plays on a bigger stage and the context that gives her power. She named some of the ten thousand, calling them "ten thousand to the tenth power." They were the women and African Americans who, like her, wanted more for themselves and their loved ones, who worked hard and fought prejudice and broke barriers like she has, who knew that freedom and opportunity were coming but didn't live to see it. "Because of them," she said, "today, I stand on solid rock. Because they were the seed, I get to be the fruit." Oprah Winfrey told us that although it looks to the rest of us like she is alone in a room full of white men, that is not her truth. And the fact that no one else can see her people with her physically does not mean they are not "really" there. They are with her in her experience, that is her truth, and no one can take it from her.

Costumes and Props

You may know you are not Oprah or the Mother of Dragons, but you can use them as inspiration for how to approach your own roles. I was not flanked by any fire-breathing dragons the day I went into that deposition, but I went in believing that truth and justice were on my side (which they were). I heard another example recently of someone who wrote the names of her supporters—family and friends who were in her corner—on a pack of Post-it notes, and went into a courtroom with those in her pocket.

The things we carry matter, whether in our minds or in our pockets. And actors use props the same way, to help them stay in touch with the reality that is most helpful to them as a way of sticking to the plot. A senior executive, for example, might carry a tablet or a Moleskine notebook or a leather binder or, more likely, nothing (powerful people tend not to carry things because others carry things for them). I have an acquaintance who works in Washington, D.C., and often testifies in Congress. On those days, he carries a thin binder with him—not a thick one—to show that he is prepared, but that most of what he needs is in his head. The binder is a prop. I loved the image of Hillary Clinton during the Benghazi hearings, looking down over her glasses and flipping through papers as though she were bored out of her mind. The things we carry affect what we do, how we interpret and respond to our circumstances, and how we play our parts.

Costumes have this effect as well. People wear clothes; actors wear costumes. It's all the same. We choose to wear the items we do, not just because they are practical, or beautiful, or stylish. Clothes, like the other items we carry on our person, are also symbolic. They convey meaning that affects other people, and that affects us as well. The things we wear and carry on our bodies reinforce shared realities about who we are to ourselves and to others. They can strengthen an unbroken line.

Some actors famously wear their costumes offstage or off-camera for this purpose—they walk and talk, literally, as if they were in the character's shoes. And when acting with power, we need to choose costumes carefully. They can help or hinder the goals we set for ourselves.

Dressing the part. When she first began work as a priest, Rev. Dr. Sara Shisler Goff was uneasy much of the time about the gravity of the character she was playing. In her parishioners' eyes, she was acting as a stand-in for God: the loftiest of roles with the weightiest of responsibilities. It was her job to be there at the most intimate, most personal moments in the lives of strangers, and to provide reassurance, meaning, and comfort. Working as a hospital chaplain one summer before she was ordained, Sara was called to the bedside of a dying parishioner. "I was the chaplain," she recalls. But she didn't much feel like one. The family was standing there, waiting, all eyes on the priest who was supposed to do what the priest is supposed to do. "They assume you've done this," she says. She hadn't. "It's not the place to say, 'This is my first time.' It was easy to get overwhelmed and think, *How am I going to do this?* I could get caught up in my head or not."

The simple act of putting on her collar helped, especially at first. It felt to her like permission to step up and play her role, and she could also sense that it put other people at ease. She found that when she was "in costume," people related to her differently, and their respect and reverence gave her permission to do what she had to do to play her role in the way that others needed.

With time and practice, she says, getting in character comes more easily. She finds she can now feel—and act—pastoral in shorts and a T-shirt if that is what is needed. "I'm in this role now and something higher takes over. You have to trust what's happening. The role is happening. If you stay present and try not to do harm, it doesn't matter what you say. Being the priest gives you permission to stay there," she says, "to stand through awkward silences, tough moments, strange encounters without having to feel self-conscious or out of place."

There are reasons for dress codes in life. Some have utilitarian value—for example, a police officer wears a loaded gun in a holster because a police officer is responsible for protecting citizens from criminals. Some police officers also wear body armor, bulletproof vests, and heavy boots, and these things weigh them down. The primary function of this equipment is, of course, to protect the officer, but it also changes the way an officer moves. A police officer in uniform moves like a silverback gorilla. When we see the officer lumbering toward us, we know right away that he is in charge. Uniforms remind people of their respective roles; they inject certainty and predictability into stressful, chaotic situations; and they remind every-one of the protocols that can keep people safe.

My female friends who are physicians tell me they never enter a room without a lab coat and a stethoscope. These are props, they tell me, that are not always needed for an actual patient visit. But many doctors believe it is helpful to carry these symbols of medical status and expertise to make the patients feel secure and to remind doctors to own their authority. It is not all for show. The things we wear on our bodies change how others respond to us, and they change us, too.

Many women who work tell me that although they would rather not wear high heels, they can't seem to give them up. Why? High heels are elevating, literally; they make a person taller and can certainly contribute to how authoritative a person looks and feels (there are famous examples of powerful men who have been known to wear heels as well, for this reason). But there are other ways heels elevate us, beyond just height. The sound of high heels hitting a hard floor, for example, announces one's arrival. Think of goose-stepping and what that conjures up. On less dramatic stages, that Washington, D.C., operative I know says he wears hard-soled shoes when he is called to testify in Congress, because the sound of his own steps on the marble floors helps to set the stage. "I like that they can hear me coming," he says; it is his way of making an entrance. The sound of his feet on the floor reminds him and everyone else that he is a force to be reckoned with. For women, high heels can be sexy, too, and there is power in that. Some women dress in ways that enhance their femininity and physical attractiveness because they believe it enhances their power, and in many cases it does. But take note: in professional contexts stilettos do not have the same effect as heels with a wider base. A woman in the former style, in terms of physics, will be easier to take down.

The term *suiting up* has entered the lexicon as a way of describing the mental preparation most professionals do when getting ready to execute something big. It's not just about looking professional; there is something about the way a suit jacket—for both men and women—squares off the body and adds breadth to the shoulders that actually makes us look physically more formidable. Sometimes it's not so much the shared reality that needs reinforcement as the private one. In situations where we need to feel and act powerful, the things we wear can give us the confidence that we look the part, and this also helps us get in character.

Owning the Space Without Owning the Land

Turf is so important for power. Animals go to great lengths to claim it, and people do too, because we know instinctively that the person who owns the space makes the rules. Jimmy Kimmel once made fun of how when President Trump sits at a table with other people, he moves things—sometimes even their things—out of the way to create more space for himself. But this impulse isn't unique to just our current president; a person I know who visited someone else in the White House during a different administration described entering a meeting where the most powerful person in the room was seated in a large, comfortable chair at the head of the table, while he himself was relegated to the far side, his puny, standard-issue chair jammed so tight against the wall he could barely slither in. Turf sends a clear signal about who has the power in a given scene.

Turf gives us permission to assert power; when we are at home, we are in charge. A meeting in your office, for example, immediately shifts the balance of power in your favor, even if you are not the most senior person in attendance. When I meet executives in a classroom at Stanford—on my turf—they raise their hands before asking me a question, even though most of them would outrank me on their turf, and some would outrank me almost anywhere else.

I'm asked often about the challenge of "owning the room." Many people think this is all about confidence and how we carry ourselves, but it is actually a question about turf. It is especially hard to own the room when you feel like a guest in someone else's house. Sometimes you will want to play power down: to defer to your "hosts" as a sign of respect, the way you might if you were a dinner guest. And other times, you will want to play power up: to take steps to own your space when you don't own the land.

Classrooms are a fascinating example. Herminia Ibarra, author of *Act Like a Leader, Think Like a Leader,* describes how she was taught as a Harvard Business School professor to establish her "territory" before the students arrived by walking the entire room, every corner, and stepping out from behind the lectern into the rest of the space. As I was learning to teach executives, I noticed at some point that, since they usually meet in the same classroom with different guest lecturers dropping in and out, I often felt like an interloper walking into "their classroom" when I showed up to teach in a program. The experience made me feel more tentative, more worried about breaking their rules, and less sure I belonged there. So I started getting into the room early, walking around, reminding myself that although I was a guest in their program, they were guests in my class. It was not a matter of lording it over anyone, but rather it gave me the opportunity to act like "the host." "Hosting" is a great way to own a room. It is welcoming and makes your guests feel honored to be there. But they are in your house. You make the rules.

Neutral turf, on the other hand, can reduce existing power imbalances. This is why many companies do "off-sites"—because they know that sometimes you need to be on neutral turf to open up lines of communication and get people to stop thinking about the status differences that divide them in the office. It's also why championship games like the Super Bowl happen someplace other than the home city of one of the participating teams, and why most big negotiations take place on neutral ground.

The type of turf matters too. Perhaps we have Harvey Weinstein to thank for the fact that most of us now understand that it's risky to host a business meeting in a hotel room. I advise my doctoral students to avoid after-dinner parties at conferences because the norms that dictate what is acceptable behavior in contexts where people go to drink and let their hair down are completely different from the norms that dictate what is acceptable in an unambiguously professional setting, or even a more wholesome daytime venue. More junior people especially are disadvantaged in these contexts because they are looking to others for cues.

Bad behavior aside, some conversations are simply better out in the open, while others are better behind closed doors. Sometimes it makes sense to play power up privately and play it down publicly. For example, a CEO might groom her successor by deferring to and praising him in public, while giving advice about what he should do differently in private. Similarly, it can be kinder and much more productive to call out a colleague's or subordinate's mistake in a small, intimate setting without a lot of people around; helping someone save face can be a generous way of playing your own power down to keep someone else from crashing. And needless to say, it is much safer for a subordinate to deliver bad news to a superior in private. On the other hand, when someone—up or down the food chain—has acted in a truly egregious way that puts others at risk, it can be important to negatively reinforce the bad behavior in public so that others understand the consequences.

When it comes to turf, the Internet is a fascinating example: it's a kind of no-man's-land in which many traditional rules of power go out the window. It is both no one's turf and everyone's turf at the same time. Consider how, in recent years, social media platforms like Facebook and Twitter have been a great equalizer. A relatively "unimportant" or "regular" person can attract a huge following—and a powerful megaphone—they would not otherwise have, based on expertise or firsthand experience. Social media also empowers people to exert influence or express opinions in ways they would not dare in face-to-face interactions: the cost of taking sides on Twitter or attacking a person with status and authority is generally much lower than in real life. This is consistent with some of the less widely publicized obedience studies by Stanley Milgram at Yale, in which participants became less and less responsive to authority figures as the physical and psychological distance between them expanded. We should not be surprised by this; studies show that people are much more likely to violate norms of appropriateness even in email, which is not anonymous. When the turf is up for grabs, it's often the most aggressive actors who win out.

The point is this: you can choose how to stage things, not just what to wear and who to be but also where to meet, to influence how the action unfolds.

Play the host. A young executive I know was delighted with the first job she landed as a newly minted MBA. At age twenty-eight, she was hired by a Fortune 500 company to come in as a regional director, tasked with turning around fifteen struggling business locations. It was a big role. Most of her direct reports were older and more experienced than she was. She was eager to get up to speed and also to establish good working relationships. So she spent the first few months meeting with all of them. They were complaining a lot, about everything. Nothing was working. And she felt she had to prove herself. So she started solving their problems for them. "I knew I could step in and do the work myself," she says, "and for a while that's what I tried to do." What she needed to learn was how to be the boss, the new sheriff in town, the person who set new standards and held them accountable for their own performance. She needed to learn how to interact with them in a way that got them focused on solving her problems—not the other way around.

She needed to play her power up, but in a way that did not put people off. We talked about it. "How can I own the room," she asked, "on their turf, without acting like a jerk?" I suggested that she try thinking of herself more as a host than a guest at the party. And she ran with it.

"I had been in the region about a year," she says, "and we had reached a point where retention and morale were at a low. I needed them to know that I needed more from them, but also that we could create a culture where teams would want to come to work despite the challenges. The idea of hosting really resonated. In normal life, when I want to build a relationship, I invite someone to my home and do something nice for them." In this case, she couldn't invite them to her home. So she tried to bring a little bit of home to them.

She ordered waffle makers and supplies, then began waking up early every morning to go into the office and start cooking. "I asked the managers to schedule their breaks so they could come off the floor to eat, and I would be there with freshly made waffles," she explained. "I would serve them, and we would sit and talk. Some of them worked through the break, they didn't want to hang out with me, I guess, but others really responded; they would come and open up and some even tried to help with the cooking. It created a real community."

She did a lot of listening, she says, and also told them what she needed from them, kindly, but in no uncertain terms. Not everyone responded right away, but in time people started coming around. "As a woman who is young and looks young, it can be tough to go into an environment with executive presence," she says. "It was a strong example that I don't have to show up like anyone else; I can use what matters to me and use that to my advantage. I was never gonna show up the way many men in the company did, but I could be genuine and caring; that is what I think a leader should be."

The Integrity Standard

When thinking about getting in role, many of us struggle with what we see as a binary choice—*I can be true to myself, or I can try to be someone else, which means doing things that are "not me."* This is how many social scientists see things; it is not how an actor thinks. Joel Podolny, my former Stanford colleague and current dean of Apple University, describes this tension as a contest between two logics: a logic of person that is defined by personality, habit, and what feels most authentic, and a logic of situation, defined by context, roles, and social norms.

Acting with power is a challenge of role-taking. And "authenticity" is not the right test. In acting, whether onstage or in life, the challenge is to find ways of telling the truth—of meaning what we say and do, even if the actions themselves are scripted. Playing *at* a role is not the same as acting; it's more like rehearsing, not doing it for real. It's relying on a script and not owning the words: like when the boss says, "My door is always open," but every time you swing by, the door is closed. Acting is a challenge of aligning the logic of the person with the logic of the situation, without either doing violence to the other. Instead of trying to be ourselves, in acting we strive to have integrity.

Integrity is "the state of being whole or undivided." It is making sure that you are 100 percent mentally and emotionally prepared to do the responsible thing—that is, what you aspire to do by virtue of your commitment to your role—no matter what is going on backstage. The goal is to bring your "true" self, including your personal experience and unique way of seeing the world, into the role, as a source of artistry, interpretation, and meaning. This means we need to ground ourselves, first, on the stage where we are standing. We need to move off ourselves—our histories, personal struggles, exhaustion, frustration, and feelings about how much attention or support we crave and how much power we do or do not "deserve"— and start tracking who we are to other people and the impact of our actions on the world around us. We need to focus more on the work we are doing than on how we look or feel while we are doing it.

Acting with power is striving for integrity by doing whatever it takes to get into a mindset that makes it possible to do the responsible thing.

When a role feels like a stretch in the theater, it's an opportunity to grow as an actor. Many actors report that they are changed forever by certain roles. The theater is one of the few situations where permission is granted to go places psychologically, physically, and emotionally that we have never gone before. In real life, new roles give us permission to use power in ways we never thought we could; they provide an opportunity to grow as a person. When you think about it this way, acting is not constraining, it is liberating, even empowering. Acting allows us to move beyond conventional views of self and open ourselves up to new ways of thinking and being.

Many of my students report that acting is addictive; after taking a class, they want to do more. They don't feel inauthentic, "stiff," or self-conscious when they are acting; they feel more real, more lost in the action, and more alive. Their interactions with one another do not feel more "staged," awkward, or disconnected; in fact, they feel more intimate. In our everyday lives, we are so focused on staying in control, on keeping our wildest, most passionate, and most vulnerable parts behind the curtain. But it takes work to keep all of that under wraps. Acting gives us permission to embrace more of ourselves, to invite a wider range of the characters who live within us to come out onstage, and in doing so, we often discover things about ourselves that we wouldn't otherwise know.

As the great playwright David Mamet puts it, an actor should strive to invent nothing but also to deny nothing. Being yourself is acting, and acting is being yourself. Once we can see this truth about social life, using power becomes much, much easier.

5

Riding Shotgun

How to Act with Power
in a Supporting Role

The specific challenges associated with getting in role vary, depending on who we are. Some people struggle to step up and play the lead; they may fear responsibility or not feel ready. But for everyone who struggles to step up, there is someone who doesn't know how to stand down. No matter who you are, everyone answers to someone. So to use power effectively, we all need to master the art of playing a supporting role. Sometimes, acting with power means putting on a bigger hat. This chapter is about how to act with power when we have to wear a smaller one.

Forgetting to Change Hats

It is easy to forget that power does not transfer automatically from one scene to another. In reality, of course, our roles are constantly shifting, and the power dynamics shift with them. To use power well, we need to take each new role seriously and choose how to play it. One executive told me that a lightbulb went off for him when I made this point in a class. About six months before, he had made a major career shift, stepping down from his role as CEO of a consulting firm and going to work for a former client's company full time. But it hadn't been going well, and now he finally knew why. "I'm still in CEO mode, telling him what I think he should do as though I know better, but now he's my boss." He laughed and shook his head. "I've got to learn how to tone it down."

This former CEO had lost the plot by acting in a way that felt natural, familiar, even authentic, but didn't fit the new story. He was doing what he always did—what had made him successful before in this relationship—rather than realizing he was playing a new part. As CEO, it seems, he had played his power up, demonstrating competence, providing direction, and behaving like "the expert," and it worked so well that his client wanted to own him. Both parties still had power, but the change in roles changed everything. To make the relationship work, he needed a new way to play it, like a shift from "head honcho" to "sidekick."

Sometimes, the role stays the same but the players change, and this requires adjusting down as well. What it means to be a good subordinate, for example, can change depending on who the boss is and how that actor likes to play it. A boss who is most comfortable playing power up is going to be most comfortable with subordinates who play power down, and a boss who prefers to play power down will find it easier to work with subordinates who can play power up. The same actions that helped you earn status with one boss can work against you with another. I learned this lesson recently, clumsily, when I acquired a new boss. My prior supervisor had been very hands off—he liked to say yes to everything, and he encouraged me to push for what I needed. If I was delivering and could make a persuasive argument, he almost never said no. So I'd learned to manage him by telling him what I wanted and why. I played my power up, and it seemed to work well for both of us. When my new boss took over, it never occurred to me that my default approach might make waves. The first time I needed something from him, we spoke on the phone briefly. I told him what I wanted and why. He said no, which, in itself, was so unexpected that it didn't really register. Undeterred, I figured he didn't understand yet how things worked. After all, he was new in his role, but I wasn't new in mine. Yikes! I cringe just thinking about it. Cheerfully, I tried again, explaining why his counteroffer was not going to work, over email. The next day, he showed up at my office unannounced, sat down on the edge of my desk, and told me to cool it. I was mortified, and said so, apologized profusely, and explained that I was following an old script. "Oh no!" I remember exclaiming, as my hands flew to my mouth, in full-on appeasement mode. "What did I do?" He explained calmly that he felt I was being too aggressive. It was his job to decide what I needed, he said; I was trying to make decisions that were above my pay grade. "I was playing by the old rules," I told him. "This is your call. And whatever you decide, I am on board."

These kinds of changes—new roles, new players—can trigger stress and insecurity in anyone. Robert Sapolsky, the Stanford biologist who studies stress responses in wild baboons, has found that even monkeys get twitchy and exhibit stress-related hormonal changes when a new actor comes onto the scene and upsets the old way of doing things. Instability within hierarchies activates deep-seated fears and insecurities that make us cling to old habits and trigger knee-jerk impulses at precisely the time when we need to consider options and try something new.

In one of my favorite essays, "On Love and Power," political scientist Hans Morgenthau wrote that the needs for love and power are two such impulses, and that they spring from the same existential well. Our biggest fears in life are about being alone or cast out of the group, and he believed, as many psychologists do, that we all seek love and power unconsciously, in varying measures, for this reason.

But especially when our fears of being cast out are heightened, these motives get triggered. When the need for love is elevated, we fear rejection and naturally try to please others to win their approval, which can actually be helpful when in a subordinate role. But when the need for power is heightened, sometimes it is because we fear we are not important enough, and this motivates behaviors that can be out of sync with role expectations.

Psychologists Delroy Paulhus and Oliver John have described this profile as a "Superhero" complex. In their study of German executives, they found that a subset of people in whom the need for power was elevated developed positive illusions about themselves to help them cope with their feelings of insecurity. The Superheroes in their study reported that rising in the ranks was a priority at work, and they presented themselves as people who were worthy of promotion. Specifically, they reported that they were both more intelligent and more socially skilled than others said they were.

When a person can't resist opportunities to elevate himself (the Superhero archetype is slightly more common in men), everyone else will feel put down, including those who actually rank higher. A Superhero (by definition) has to save the day, by rescuing others from their own incompetence and vulnerability, in order to feel powerful. He does whatever it takes—giving unsolicited advice, claiming expertise in all topics, name-dropping, disagreeing with anyone who seems to know more, reminding others of his accomplishments.

So you can see how having a Superhero complex might present challenges when playing a subordinate role. A Superhero needs to land on top and, as a result, struggles to stand down, step aside, or wait in the wings. The fear of being unimportant, undervalued, or underestimated can make it very hard to resist trying to steal the show.

Misreading the Room

I once interviewed a job candidate who showed up without the materials I asked him to bring and then actually leaned back and put his feet up on my desk. Hard to imagine, isn't it? I think he was trying to bond with me by showing that we were "in the same club," but it had the opposite effect. It is one thing to believe you are qualified for a big role or that you trust your own potential for growth; it is another to pretend you are on equal footing with the casting director. Similarly, while it is one thing to sit down in a job interview with confidence and an open physical posture, it is another thing entirely to walk in acting as if you own the place: being too relaxed, too buddy-buddy with the interviewer; trying to hijack the agenda; or worse, talking down to the interviewer (or putting your feet up on her desk) to show how comfortable you are, how much respect you deserve, and how perfect you are for the role.

We've all—particularly women—heard the advice that we need to claim a seat at the table. And this is generally good advice, with one caveat: you have to belong in that seat, and at that table. All seats in all rooms are not created equal, and no assistant has ever gained status by plopping down in the boss's chair. Similarly, the conventional advice to speak up in a meeting to earn respect, or avoid being marginalized, only works if the things you say, or the fact that you are speaking, adds value for the others in the room. If you haven't earned the status already, if there is no real need to hear from you at this time, and you don't have something useful to say, this strategy will almost certainly backfire. As a simple rule of thumb, you will almost never earn status for speaking more simply because you feel self-conscious about the fact that you haven't been speaking enough.

Acting as if you have more power than you do is a rookie mistake.

And it's perfectly understandable. People watch a TED Talk about doing "power poses" in private to prepare for a big meeting, presentation, or interview and infer that once they get in the room, they need to act with bravado to make a good impression. But acting "as if" in this way is not a winning strategy. You want to act with awareness of the power you actually have, by virtue of the role you are actually playing, not the power you fear you will lose if you show someone else the respect to which they are entitled by virtue of the role they are in.

Recently, a colleague told me he had "overshot" when he was called in to do some coaching for a group of executives. As he was about to begin speaking, he noticed that the highest-ranking client in the room had his eyes glued to his phone. To get his attention, my colleague stood at the front of the room staring at the client pointedly, without speaking, the way a stern grade school teacher might. It was an attempt to regain control of the room, but it was also a gross miscalculation of the power dynamics between a consultant and a client. He overestimated his status, lost the plot, and ended up losing the client.

In the abstract, we tend to worry more about the costs of underestimating where we rank in a group than overestimating where we rank, but this is a miscalculation. In a study by psychologist and social-hierarchy expert Cameron Anderson, members of student work groups who overestimated their social rank—specifically, reporting that they ranked higher than their teammates said they did—were not only disliked; their collaborators downgraded their contributions to the work effort, saying they should be paid less than those whose status beliefs were more carefully calibrated. Showing someone else more respect than you have to is a relatively safe error. But you can't play your own power up without playing someone else's power down. Showing too little respect for a highly respected person in the group suggests you don't know your place, which can be extremely costly, like committing social suicide. This is why playing power up all the time doesn't work.

There is something uniquely off-putting about people who act as if they are more important than they are. But why? For one, when you overshoot in this way, it sends a message to other people about how you see yourself relative to how you see them. It tells your superiors you don't think they deserve the power and status they have earned. It tells your peers you think you are better than they are. It's like spewing insults at everyone around. The inability to read a room is a real liability, a red flag for potential employers, clients, and pretty much anyone, in pretty much any context. It suggests you care too much about yourself and how you look onstage, and not enough about how anyone else looks.

My daughter once had the honor of meeting Supreme Court justice Ruth Bader Ginsburg while on a class trip to Washington, D.C. She later described the horror she experienced when one of her eighth-grade classmates interrupted Justice Ginsburg by shouting, "Could you speak up, we can't hear you back here!" A thirteen-year-old could perhaps be forgiven for not realizing that although you have been encouraged to use your voice in the classroom, one does not bark orders at a U.S. Supreme Court justice, no matter where you are. I heard this story only because the kids who were in the room where it happened were talking about it in incredulous voices while riding in the back of my minivan. If eighth-graders could sense that this behavior was "off," why are some full-grown adults so oblivious when it comes to reading the room?

We often lose track of hierarchical norms when the logic of person overwhelms the logic of situation: when the cues we are getting from inside ourselves are just too noisy. It is natural to feel anxious or insecure when we feel that the stakes are high and our status is on the line, but the anxiety that arises in these situations can trigger impulses that may not be appropriate for someone in your role.

Whenever I talk about Superheroes in class, some show up later in my office. These students know who they are. They tell me, "I always get feedback that I'm too competitive, too aggressive, and arrogant. I don't mean to be, but when I'm criticized or feel put down for some reason, I can't accept it. I have to win the argument." One Superhero student of mine described an incident in a class when he was role-playing a young start-up founder who was making a pitch to members of his board—played by real executives who were visiting that day. He'd spent hours and hours preparing, and now, unexpectedly, "his board" fired him on the spot. "It was bad," he told me. "I fought with them, demanded an explanation, insisted it was unfair, and tried to prove they were wrong." In the moment, he wanted to show the grace, resilience, and decorum befitting a CEO. But instead, he threw a tantrum.

Play a Supporting Role

It is common to think of hierarchical roles as a choice between leading and following. But this is not how groups actually function. Groups function when those in supporting roles see themselves as partners to those who rank above them. This requires acknowledging that in a supporting role, you are needed, and that gives you power, which comes with its own responsibilities. When you get into a vehicle, you can climb into the way, way back, take your eyes off the road, and fight with the other kids about who has more space. Or, you can choose the passenger seat and imagine yourself riding shotgun. It requires a different level of commitment, and the willingness to put someone else first.

Riding shotgun is incompatible with using your role as a stepping-stone to something bigger and better for you. It is hard to truly live in a role when you view it as an opportunity to get somewhere else.

An executive I know deals with this all the time. Often he finds that people who seek specific roles within the large, high-profile organization he leads do so less because they want to serve the organization or advance its mission and more because they want to be associated with the brand, create a personal platform, build a résumé, and become more visible as a mover and shaker. Many books on power will tell you this is the right way to think about power. I have always thought it was nonsense. Everyone knows when this happens. These people have not just lost the plot, they never cared about the plot to begin with. Organizations and roles are not resources to be consumed just for personal advancement (except maybe in our own minds). They are opportunities to contribute to something more important than personal advancement, and, maybe sometimes, to be recognized for that.

We all want to impress others, earn their respect, and advance professionally. And we worry sometimes that playing a smaller role will make us look small, weak, or unimportant.

But having the confidence to sit quietly while someone else gets applause is as much a source of power as the ability to seize the spotlight. In his book *Powers of Two,* Joshua Wolf Shenk observes that many of history's most important innovations, although often attributed to the efforts of a lone genius, are actually the work of pairs—John Lennon and Paul McCartney, Steve Jobs and Steve Wozniak, and Bill Gates and Paul Allen, for example—that "have one member in the spotlight and another offstage." "The irony is that, while our eyes naturally follow the star, a pair's center of gravity is often with the one we see less," writes Shenk.

Focus on the Craft

For everyone who craves the spotlight, there are always people who relish doing work behind the scenes. David Litt, one of President Obama's top speechwriters, whose specialty was writing jokes and one-liners into the president's speeches, describes how in the first term, the president did not even know his name. "It was not like an episode of *The West Wing*," he says. "I never had a 'walk and talk.' I was one of the people giving a piece of paper to someone in the walk and talk and then scurrying out of the frame," he told *The New York Times*. "I didn't make a ton of history, and that's totally fine."

The ability to stay focused on the work, on the craft, on the higher-order objectives—even if it comes at the expense of our own personal glory—affords tremendous power. Whether that role is as a presidential staffer, a mentor, a coach, an advisor, a partner, a chief operating officer, or anything else, playing a supporting role requires the humility, flexibility, and confidence to cede the spotlight to someone else. You have to take pride in doing whatever it takes to make someone else look good. Lisa Fischer, the Rolling Stones' longtime backup singer, for example, is not your typical groupie. She describes how, in her audition with Mick Jagger, she put in her demo tape and started singing, and he started doing his thing— waving his arms, dancing, and gyrating around her. But she was unfazed, unmoved, just stuck with the music—and that helped her seal the deal. "Some people will do anything to be famous," she told *The New York Times*. "I just wanted to sing."

When you focus on doing the work, on perfecting your craft, it suggests that you care more about your contribution to the group outcome than about how much recognition you receive. It signals clearly that you care more about the art than about being known as the artist. And this is especially important for building trust while in a supporting role.

Roles exist to advance collective causes. When we accept a job, we are being paid to put the organization first. The roles we play are not "ours"; we don't own them and we don't take them with us. We merely occupy them for a period of time. The goal should not be to do whatever it takes to amass personal power, wealth, and fame. We gain power—and maybe eventually wealth and fame—only through making ourselves useful by influencing others' outcomes in a positive way. If we also move up as a result of these actions, that is great. But I'm pretty sure that framing all of our choices in terms of what will elevate us as individuals almost always works against our goals.

Many people resist taking roles that don't feel like enough of a step up. But this focus on status and advancement can cost them great opportunities to be part of something meaningful. Sheryl Sandberg describes how she almost missed the boat (or the rocket ship) when she was invited by then CEO Eric Schmidt to join Google in 2001. She was worried the role wasn't big enough and that she might be taking a step back instead of forward. Schmidt told her, "When you are offered a seat on a rocket ship, you don't ask which seat, you just get on." She did, and never looked back. She says it was some of the best advice she was ever given. What is fulfilling, in life, is to serve a higher purpose in roles where you can have real impact— not just the ones that look good on a résumé.

Take One for the Team

When we are in a subordinate role, every action can feel risky. But a willingness to take personal risk for the good of the group is the most reliable source of status there is. When our actions show that we care about others, that we are ready to sacrifice our own interests to advance others' interests, we earn others' trust. When our actions show that we care more about our own interests than what is best for the group, trust and status are depleted.

It is not so much a question of caring or not caring about other people and the groups we belong to—I believe most people do care—it is a question of whether we are able to show we care. And showing we care ultimately comes down to a question of sacrifice: How much are you willing to risk losing in order for others to win? How much skin do you have in the game? This is hard to fake.

To play a supporting role effectively, we can play power up or down, but to be helpful and build trust, we have to stay connected to what is happening in the here and now, to show that we are listening and paying attention to what is most important to others. We have to seize the moment to take a risk that has the potential to benefit the whole ensemble. To do this, we have to stay connected to what is happening onstage and to see ourselves as part of it.

The best example I can think of to illustrate this point is from something I witnessed at work. We have a tradition at Stanford called the "Executive Challenge"—during which all 470-some first-year MBA students perform, en masse, in a series of role-playing exercises with alumni who show up for the day.

The students arrive on the day of the challenge and meet a group of distinguished alumni who have flown in from all over the world for this activity. They are given a business case, and have about an hour to prepare. They play businesspeople (e.g., entrepreneur, team lead), and the alumni play the stakeholders (e.g., board members, venture capitalists, customers, and clients). The goal is to strike a deal at the end of a half-hour meeting.

These meetings take place in front of a panel of judges—alumni and faculty volunteers—who score six different pairs of students in different versions of the same meeting throughout the day. The students have to pitch solutions to problems and wrangle the numbers, while also managing themselves, each other, and especially the alumni in the room, who are not there to make it easy for them. It's a simulation, of course, but the stakes are high. The students' teammates are watching, their professors are watching, and they are interacting with alumni who could turn out to be business contacts in the future. They are making first impressions. What they do, in role, counts. Their instincts will reveal what they bring to the role, or who they are as actors.

In general, the students show up very well. They are mostly like you'd expect: smart, bright-eyed, and sometimes rough around the edges. Some look like they are wearing their parents' suits. They are scared, understandably, and some are more successful at hiding it than others. I've been impressed on more than one occasion. But one year, a student did something that knocked my socks off. She defined for me what it meant to use power in a supporting role.

My memory for this incident is more like a snapshot than a full-length film. I know there are two students in the front of the room, but I only see one, a dark-skinned African American woman. She is small and pretty, in a navy-blue suit. Everything around her is a blur. I see a couple of the alumni—mostly white guys—across the table, some with their backs to me, others in profile. They are expensively dressed and a little rambunctious, bouncing back in their chairs, ready to pounce with tough questions. She is in the center, calm but alive, like the eye of a storm. Everything spins around her.

She has a partner who is also animated; he is doing a lot of the talking. She is more quiet, but not silent, and still, but not frozen. She does not look afraid. Her energy is focused. Her face is relaxed. When she smiles, I can see the whites of her teeth.

One of the executives is pitched forward suddenly, moving in on them. "What if you're wrong," he shouts, waving his hands. "What if it fails? Who is going to take responsibility?"

The students are not expecting this question.

"Who's the point person on this?" he demands.

This throws the woman's partner off; he shifts and glances in her direction, and without flinching, she speaks. "You come to me."

I get goosebumps just writing about it. She stopped everyone cold, left them speechless. The power in the room went to her. The alumni settled down, sat back in their chairs. No more questions. Her partner exhaled. With that one line, she told them she would accept responsibility for whatever risk they were taking and that she would, and could, have their backs. They were sold. The deal was done.

The team reached an agreement with minutes to spare. The other teams that day mostly ran out of time before even getting to make a request. The woman and her partner shook everyone's hand and left the room. And the executives, their eyes like saucers, acknowledged to one another that they had seen something special. In her feedback session, I recall that we gushed about her performance but had trouble articulating what, exactly, had made it so powerful.

She was not the loudest actor; she was not trying to be the smartest person in the room. She was not the most controlling, the scariest, or the most outgoing. She was not schmoozing, showing off, or even getting most of the attention. But she was entirely present. Her energy was focused and contained. She was patient, disciplined, and completely in control of herself. And she was obviously listening. Against a backdrop of others wrestling and jockeying for status, she looked like the grown-up in the room. She was not looking to be a player. She was looking to make a difference. Yes, it was a role-taking exercise. But her performance was inspired and unforgettable, and it revealed something profound about her instincts.

In an individualistic world, where it is considered normal to fight for status and attention, and where self-advocacy is thought to be the best way of attaining success, this actor distinguished herself by doing the opposite. Her actions said, *I'm here for you, and whatever happens, I can handle it: You come to me.* She stepped between the big guns in the room and their fears. She knew what they needed, while her teammates did not. And when her partner hesitated to put himself in the crosshairs, for whatever reason, she took one for the team. She stepped up and claimed status without permission, but she did it at a time and in a way that took care of everyone else. She stood out because she was all in.

In the theater, casting directors look for many things. Commitment to the role is one of them. It helps to have a record of good performance. It helps to have a good reputation—that is, good buzz, the kind that comes from having worked well with others and respected professional norms of conduct in previous productions. It helps to have the right look—but that's not the most important thing. Great actors steal scenes by playing the parts in which they are cast, however small, with complete and total commitment, in riveting, personal, and unforgettable ways. To use power well, it is not enough to step in front of the camera just long enough for a close-up. We have to be all in, look for opportunities to make a difference, and do whatever it takes, whether it elevates us in that moment or not. This, at least in part, is how we win bigger roles in the future.

6

The Show Must Go On

Making an Entrance and Owning the Spotlight

I t's human nature, supposedly, to be interested in power: not just to find it interesting but to be drawn to power, to crave more, to seek it for oneself. The German philosopher Friedrich Nietzsche was one of the first to describe this motive; he called it "the will to power." Nietzsche believed that we naturally approach each and every life circumstance by striving to attain the highest possible position. This kind of striving is healthy, and even necessary, he believed, to justify the existence of humankind.

But the idea of having power is, for many people, more attractive than the reality. My colleagues and I like to joke that although we want to be offered the biggest jobs in our respective fields, we aren't sure we want to do them. Many people in many situations are more comfortable in the wings than in the spotlight, and many of us would rather be loved than feared.

Performance anxiety, especially in a big role, can be a really big deal. In the mid-1990s I was teaching organizational behavior in the evening program at Northwestern's Kellogg School of Management. The students were managers who came to class after a full day's work. They were exhausted but also energized by the opportunity to take a step back and think about the challenges they were facing in their jobs.

One year, to spark a discussion about the impact of organizational roles, I decided to show a clip from the famous Stanford prison experiment conducted in 1971 by Philip Zimbardo to study the psychological effects of power. College students who had signed up to take part in a mock prison scenario—staged in the basement of the Stanford psychology department—were randomly assigned to play the role of either prisoner or guard for a period of two weeks, while Zimbardo (in the role of superintendent) and his research assistants watched.

Some of the outcomes of this experiment are widely known. In recent years, the psychological torture inflicted by some of the "guards" has been likened to the prisoner abuse that was discovered at Abu Ghraib. Things got so ugly that the experiment was called off after only six days.

Before showing a clip of the footage in class, I asked my students (all of whom had experience as managers) to put themselves in the participants' shoes. I asked them to imagine that they themselves had been assigned to the job of prison guard and were to report for work for the first time the next day. "What would you be thinking?" I asked.

I can't recall what I expected them to say, but I assumed that whatever it was would provide an interesting window into how power could turn normal people into abusive tormentors. They were quiet for a bit.

"I'd be scared," one finally admitted.

"Of what?" I asked, thinking perhaps that he'd misunderstood the exercise. "You would be in charge."

Then others chimed in. They wanted to do a good job but weren't sure they could be successful. They were supposed to keep things under control but weren't allowed to use force. The prisoners were not going to be happy with the arrangement; what if they refused to comply? The guards had no real power beyond their formal "guard" titles, and they feared the prisoners would see it. As they anticipated showing up as prison guards, their fear of being seen through was palpable. In essence, they had performance anxiety, and they said it put them on edge.

Marc Andreessen, the legendary venture capitalist and founder of the early Internet browser Netscape, has famously said there are only two reactions to actually being the person in charge of a startup: euphoria and terror. And as anyone who likes roller coasters will tell you, it can be hard to tell the difference. The Stanford prison study has been held up for decades as the classic example of how people become drunk or giddy with power and is cited as "proof" that the typical reaction to power is to abuse the powerless for fun. But there was no sign of this mentality in my students when I asked them to imagine being there in the role of prison guard. What came to mind for them ahead of time was fear.

Fear and Three Ways to Play It

It's typically assumed that the guards in the Stanford prison study were callous, cruel, even sadistic by nature. And it's true that some guards dealt with the pressure to perform by doing whatever they could to break the prisoners down—everything from degrading them verbally, to taking away their mattresses and leaving them to sleep on the hard concrete, to locking them in "solitary confinement." These behaviors were widely publicized. But what is less widely known about the Stanford prison study is that not all of the guards reacted this way. In fact, according to reports of the study, the guards used their power in three distinct ways, and they emerged in equal numbers.

The Aggressors. When interviewed about it in the years since, what those guards who abused the "prisoners" have described in various ways wasn't the desire to harm, but rather the desire to do a good job. In one recent interview, a participant recalled wanting to deliver the results he thought Zimbardo wanted: to demonstrate how power leads to abuse. These guards played their power up by doing whatever they could to make sure the prisoners felt maximally helpless, so they could stay in control as they had been directed. But their motivations were grounded in the desire to win approval from the researchers and prove themselves to their peers—to be "the best" at what they had been asked to do—not to coerce and harm others gratuitously. They wanted to excel in their roles, and they did whatever it took.

The Bureaucrats. While some guards went "above and beyond" what might have been expected, "showing off" for the experimenter just how well they could control the prisoners, some guards simply tried to match expectations (as opposed to aspirations) perfectly. They tried to follow the rules to a T and to do exactly as they had been asked, no less and no more. These guards played it straight—they were highly conscientious and were described by the researchers as firm but fair. They defined performing well as doing the job "correctly."

In contrast to those who overplayed it by taking personal risks to show creativity and initiative, those who played it straight were risk averse; they were less concerned with "crushing it" than with "dotting *i*'s and crossing *t*'s." They played their roles by abdicating their power; they were just following orders.

The Appeasers. There was another group of guards in the Stanford prison study whose behavior is not widely discussed. Instead of playing dirty or playing it straight, they played nice. They tried to appease and befriend the prisoners by doing them favors and giving them special treats. They wanted to keep the prisoners "fat and happy," so that the prisoners would like them and, presumably, not revolt.

These three responses to performance anxiety among the guards in the Stanford prison study are not unlike what we see in other studies of power and leadership. Some people play their power up, some play it down, and some play it straight. But each of these responses is a different way of dealing with the performance anxiety that comes with a high-power role.

It is not intuitive that people feel scared when stepping up in their lives. But as many know, one of the great ironies of power is that we seek leading roles in order to feel more secure and more in control, but then the joke is on us: we find that the moment we step into a powerful position is the moment we realize how little control we actually have. As any parent, any manager, any team leader knows, stepping into a position of power while feeling unsure of your ability to control things is a nightmare, literally, as in: I'm trying to get to class on time and I'm stuck between floors in an elevator, I can't find my classroom, I am completely unprepared or have prepared the wrong subjects, or I'm standing in front of the room trying to start class and the students are coming and going as if I'm not even there. These are all nightmares I have actually had.

It's not just about control, of course. It is the prospect of bombing on a big stage. Mostly, we imagine that the occupants of high-power roles feel less performance pressure than the rest of us. But once we can see power up close, from the perspective of the role occupant, it doesn't look this way at all.

Power and Performance Anxiety

From one day to the next, you may go from being on the team to being the one leading it. You may move from sidekick to head honcho. You will not feel like a different person, but power changes everything. In all likelihood, you will not feel any more powerful than you did yesterday, but to others, you are not the same person. A powerful role attracts attention, big audiences, and often harsh reviews. It comes with responsibility and great expectations, and it sometimes sparks envy and resentment. Stepping into a bigger role lands us on a bigger stage, where, inevitably, we feel smaller. And in the glare of the spotlight, we feel exposed, naked, with our weakness on display.

In the management world, the specific fear that accompanies stepping into a big role is described as *imposter syndrome*. It is a form of performance anxiety that affects all kinds of actors who find themselves playing roles for which they do not feel fully equipped. Imposter syndrome is a fear of exposing oneself, of "breaking the line" in Stanislavski's terms, and revealing the gap between the actor and the role in which he has been cast. It is a fear of being seen through, like the Wizard of Oz ("Pay no attention to that man behind the curtain!") or the emperor with no clothes.

We've all been there: thrust into a role for which we feel just barely qualified, in which we are supposed to act with authority, and unsure we can perform as expected. A psychiatrist I know who works in Cambridge, Massachusetts (near Harvard), claims to have counseled Nobel Prize winners who suffer from this affliction. And a professor I know, long-tenured by now, still viscerally recalls how, early in his career, his inner imposter got away from him in the most literal way possible. He had offered to teach a class on writings by three canonical thinkers: Marx, Nietzsche, and Freud. He knew their works inside and out, and yet he kept accidentally referring to the course he was teaching as "Marx, Nietzsche, and *Fraud*."

Imposter syndrome is a fear of being exposed, and sometimes, as this Freudian slip illustrates perfectly, we react by exposing ourselves. It's a classic if subconscious choice to play power down, like showing your jugular, as in "Please don't bite me. I'm not worth it." Responses to imposter syndrome often take this form, but not always. Some people, instead of taking themselves down, will take themselves out, by hiding, freezing, or losing their voice. Others play power up in response to imposter syndrome; they try to hide their weakness by acting more superior than necessary. The classic response is to overprepare, to train for the role by beefing up knowledge, expertise, and confidence, and then wait too long before making an entrance. When we step into a big role without techniques for managing performance anxiety, these impulses can all work against us, in a number of ways.

Fear of Not Measuring Up

When the goal is to establish trust in a high-power role, the fear of appearing incompetent can distract us from what matters more, which is the degree to which our subordinates believe we have their best interests at heart. It's not intuitive, but research on this point is clear: the competence of a high-power actor is usually taken for granted. The bigger problem, usually, is learning how to demonstrate that we care.

I am often contacted by friends, colleagues, and former students after a big promotion. They want advice about how to introduce themselves to the people they are going to oversee, and usually they don't want to make an entrance until they feel like they know what they are doing. They want to get the lay of the land, learn the culture and politics, and decide which initiatives to prioritize and which stances to adopt. Often, they don't know yet how they plan to address important challenges and fear showing up without answers. But waiting too long to make an appearance, or only making an appearance—that is, trying to "get in and get out"—has unique downsides for a high-power actor.

It has been argued that President George W. Bush lost many of his supporters after Hurricane Katrina, when he waited too long to go to Louisiana to assess the damage, and then drew even more criticism when he flew over the disaster in a plane instead of meeting on the ground with his constituents. Contrast this to how Mayor Rudy Giuliani was hailed nationally for standing amid the rubble of the World Trade Center on September 11, wearing a hard hat. When you are the person in charge, you have to show up, even if it means getting dirty or putting yourself in harm's way. The fact that Bush seemed to be keeping his distance from the Katrina tragedy, not offering to help personally, or hiding from his responsibility to help, made him look callous, even hostile, toward the victims (even though he wasn't actively doing harm). Famously, Bush was photographed looking out the window of his plane as he flew over the devastation, and although he has since reported feeling deeply concerned about what he saw, and aides have explained that he wanted to avoid diverting attention and resources away from the rescue effort, somehow that was not how his actions read to the rest of the world.

The lesson is this: when you are the person in charge, people will look to you for many things. Mostly, they will be trying to figure out how important they are to you. As the person in the high-power role, you are the harbinger of everyone else's self-worth. You must make it a priority to show people they are worthy of your time and attention, because as the person in the high-power role, you will be the beneficiary of many privileges. But on this, you will not receive the benefit of the doubt.

Recently I talked with a friend who had been promoted into a C-suite position at a tech company whose product was a path-breaking innovation that was poised to create a new market and was generating a lot of buzz. The only problem was that she had no idea how the exciting new product worked. On one hand, she wanted to jump right in and help her team adjust to their new reality. And on the other hand, she did not want them to decide she wasn't technically up to snuff. Should she consider adjusting her default management style as she moved into a much bigger role in a totally unfamiliar industry? Wisely, she had negotiated for a few weeks before starting so she could get up to speed on the technology and the industry she was entering. Her inclination was to take some time to learn about the people, too, before having any meetings with her team.

"Don't wait," I told her. "The most important thing is to just be there. Meet with everyone right away, even if you don't know what you are going to tell them. Find out how they are doing and what their hopes and concerns are. You may not make the perfect entrance, but you will get points for showing you care and are interested in what matters to them. They need to be able to look you in the eye and see that they are a priority for you, that you respect and are eager to learn from them, and that you are paying attention. Don't hide out until you feel ready. That is step one."

So you have to show up physically, but as even the most seasoned performers will tell you, being there physically does not guarantee a great performance. The fear of bombing on a big stage can afflict even the most seasoned performers among us. Jay-Z (Shawn Corey Carter), the famous rapper and record producer, describes how he choked during his first live show. "I just forgot the words," says Carter. "I stood there, and I tried to pass the mic to Damon Dash, who I co-founded Roc-A-Fella with. I gave him the mic, like, 'here.' He was like, 'man, I don't rap!' I just didn't know what to do. I didn't—I was just, like, in shock."

Similarly, the legendary singer-songwriter Patti Smith has talked about having been uncharacteristically overcome with stage fright, despite her decades of experience performing, while honoring Bob Dylan at his televised Nobel Prize award event in Sweden. Dylan himself had declined the invitation; he did not even want to be there. So Smith agreed to perform in his stead. A renowned poet, lyricist, and performance artist in her own right, Smith had been chosen to perform at the ceremony for exactly these reasons. Yet when the moment arrived, she became incapable of singing.

"The opening chords of the song were introduced, and I heard myself singing," she wrote. "The first verse was passable, a bit shaky, but I was certain I would settle. But instead I was struck with a plethora of emotions, avalanching with such intensity that I was unable to negotiate them. From the corner of my eye, I could see the huge boom stand of the television camera, and all the dignitaries upon the stage and the people beyond. Unaccustomed to such an overwhelming case of nerves, I was unable to continue. I hadn't forgotten the words that were now a part of me. I was simply unable to draw them out." In short, Smith "choked." She was so far out of her comfort zone, she became momentarily incapable of doing what she came to do.

Often, before a big meeting or presentation, a speaker will say, "I just want to get through it." This is also a response to the fear of showing weakness and the anxiety that comes with performing. Many executives manage their discomfort with power and their fear of not doing power "right" by "checking out," or "phoning it in," which is a version of the same thing. We figure if we don't really show up, we can't really screw up. And then we wonder why subordinates don't trust us. If you can't find a way to be present, it shows that you don't want to be there. And because you are the person in charge, no one is going to assume it is because you care too much about them, even if that is the reason.

This holds true whether we are in charge or not. In big meetings, we've all noticed those people who engage in side conversations while others have the floor. They may have shown up in body, but in spirit they aren't all there. Instead of staying in touch with the reasons they care about the event and its outcomes, which can make performance anxiety worse, they pretend they are participating, but in reality they are going through the motions, sitting there, playing at the role of participant, while watching, judging, and letting others do the heavy lifting. They aren't sure they want to risk saying what they are thinking in front of the whole group, so instead, they behave like spectators at a sporting event, commenting on the action from the sidelines. Without taking that personal risk of showing up for everyone, it is hard to be seen as a valued member of the team.

Fear of Responsibility

In contrast to Nietzsche, who believed everyone wants to rank first, psychologists Sigmund Freud and Erich Fromm argued that, actually, most people fear power and try to avoid accountability for using it. Many executives deal with this anxiety by acting just like the "bureaucrats" in the Stanford prison experiment; that is to say, they play it by the book. They try to follow the rules, to refer to existing policies, principles, and higher-ranking people instead of owning responsibility for their own decisions.

A pertinent (if fictional) example of this plays out in the British film *Eye in the Sky*, as two inexperienced drone pilots sit in a bunker in Nevada, waiting for the order to launch a drone that will kill a suicide bomber in a residential neighborhood in Nairobi, Kenya. British colonel Katherine Powell (played by Helen Mirren) wants to launch the missile attack, but she can't get anyone to approve it—no one wants to be held accountable. First, she consults her legal counsel, who recommends she ask her lieutenant general, who is supervising the mission. But the British cabinet needs to agree, and no one wants to be the one to say yes—so the lieutenant general refers up to the foreign secretary, who then tries to defer to the U.S. secretary of state, who is on what appears to be a diplomatic visit to China. In a moment of comic relief, the U.S. secretary of state authorizes the attack immediately, in the middle of a Ping-Pong game, as though it is a no-brainer. In the end, the hawkish colonel finds a way to get her missile launched, but only after going around a veritable army of high-powered decision makers who have more power than she does but do not want to be held accountable if the mission goes badly.

For many people—even most people, as it turns out—the fear of accountability is so profound that when push comes to shove, they'd rather not make the big calls themselves. They may want to be in the room where it happens, but they try to avoid that seat at the head of the table.

You may assume that most people will always prefer winning over being the runner-up. Yet in research led by my colleague and PhD student Em Reit, we find that, on average, most people (slightly more than half, across studies) report they would rather rank second than first. The reason, she speculates, is that people like to maximize status in groups but avoid being responsible for using power. In short, the accountability that comes with ranking first in groups is, for many, not worth it.

When the goal is to seek status but avoid responsibility, we tend to take actions that reinforce the status quo. This is not necessarily a bad thing, but coloring inside the lines is not always associated with leadership potential or perceptions of "greatness" in a high-power role.

Fear of Upward Contempt

Most people fear doing things that provoke hostility in others, most of the time. And using power poses special risks in this department, particularly for those with an elevated need to be liked. The occupants of high-power roles are targets of envy and resentment, almost by definition, according to political scientist William Ian Miller, who describes "upward contempt" as an inevitable feature of hierarchical life. When we are consumed with winning a popularity contest, it can be hard to use power well.

I recently spoke with a group of board members and learned how common this is. The CEO of a private equity firm approached me afterward and said, "I think you have hit on one of the biggest HR challenges in our firm. We bring in all of these associates, and the best of them get promoted. They are superstars with numbers, on a steep trajectory upward, and then they stumble. They can't handle being promoted above their peers; they want to pretend they are all still equal. Suddenly they have to hold their friends accountable, and they want to pretend it's not their job! We've lost a lot of good performers this way. And the groups they manage start to unravel. They don't trust that anyone is in charge. It brings out the worst in everyone."

David Winter, the political psychologist who studied the impact of elevated needs among U.S. presidents and how it affected their behavior while in office, writes that Richard Nixon was the classic example of a powerful person who let his need to be liked get the best of him. His attempts to spy on Democratic Party officials by wiretapping the Democratic headquarters were driven, according to Winter, by an intense paranoia that stemmed from his fear that he was viewed as a low-status outsider in Washington and that the insiders were out to get him. It's a narrative that has come back around.

Channeling Fear into a Powerful Performance

In short, performance anxiety is a normal part of stepping into a bigger role. Even professional actors experience stage fright at times. But they learn to expect and even welcome the surge of nervous energy that arrives before a performance, because they have techniques for harnessing that energy and using it in constructive ways.

Keep calm and carry on. At its most basic level, anxiety is a physiological response, and you can address the physical aspects on their own terms. Athletes, dancers, musicians, and, of course, actors manage performance anxiety by engaging in a physical warm-up before showtime that reminds the body of what it is there to do. They stretch, loosen up, try to move the energy through their bodies instead of trying to block it or make it go away. A physical warm-up is a way of shaking off emotional baggage, releasing familiar ways of holding the body, letting go of what just happened, and creating space within the body for physical flexibility, agility, and adaptation.

There are many ways to warm up before a performance, and because the actors I teach with all use different methods, I've tried it all.

It helps first to learn to recognize what anxiety feels like. I learned to do this from Kay Kostopoulos, my first acting teacher. "Close your eyes and check in with yourself," she says. "How are you standing? Where is your chin? How is your weight distributed? Do you feel light or heavy? What is going on in your head?" It's a personal inventory, as she describes it, and I've come to understand this process as a way of noticing not just the feelings I'm experiencing and the body language I'm exhibiting in the here and now, but also the baggage I have brought with me from elsewhere. Anxiety is energy; it feels like a motor, and you can almost hear it whirring in your ears, blocking out other sounds. I feel it in my face, in a clenched jaw, a frozen smile, or a knit brow, and in my chest, shoulders, and hands, which are sometimes clenched for no reason. And I feel it in my breath—which may be shallow, or even held, temporarily. In my mind, these natural responses to fear and anxiety are my body's attempts to block the energy I'm generating or shut it down.

When I feel these physical sensations, I've learned I can just focus on releasing the tension and trying to move the energy through my body. A psychologist I know who treats anxiety once told me that she reminds her patients that anxiety is like a wave; it comes and it passes. Instead of trying to block it or turn it off, she recommends trying to help it move through. Sometimes I step outside the room where I'll be performing and just walk around, shake out my hands, blow air through my lips, and physically stretch. If I jump up and down, exerting myself a little, my breath will change—I'll start taking deep, relaxing breaths instead of short, shallow ones. A physical warm-up moves the energy and the blood from the head into the body, and when I do these things, when I know my body is ready to act, the fear starts to feel more like excitement.

A physical warm-up can also help you appear more relaxed when you are feeling tense and is great preparation for any kind of performance: a big presentation to a client, a meeting with your boss, an interview, or a virtual meeting, whether on or off camera. I recently did some coaching with executives who were role-playing an important conversation. I saw a lot of blinking, twitching, trembling, fake smiles, and eyebrows flailing. I asked the actors to stretch out their faces—as I have learned to do—to open them first as wide as possible and then scrunch them up as tightly as possible, and then to relax the face muscles, and the tics all disappeared. Part of the magic of a physical warm-up for me is that it helps to focus on acting, or doing something, instead of on what I am feeling. In general, it helps to free your mind from thoughts about how you are performing so you can focus on doing more important things.

Rehearse. In almost every endeavor, practice makes perfect. That's because performing a desired action over and over again turns it into a habit, or what psychologists call a *dominant response*. Studies of *social facilitation* find that the presence of an audience tends to increase the likelihood of the dominant response in all kinds of tasks. So it is important to rehearse this response before the audience is present. Otherwise, you will fall back on those other, less helpful well-learned responses.

The presence of an audience can enhance all kinds of performances, if the habit that gets triggered is the correct one. Experienced athletes, for example, often perform better in front of an audience, because the anxiety is a source of physical strength and, importantly, because experienced athletes (and other performers) know where to focus when anxiety kicks in. Inexperienced performers, on the other hand, tend to get rattled by an audience, because they don't know what to do with the excess energy. And in these situations, the presence of an audience makes things worse.

Actors and athletes aren't the only ones who have to be ready to channel their energy when the pressure is on. For all kinds of professionals, especially those who are responsible for protecting others in high-stakes situations, practice is a necessary discipline. Police, firefighters, EMTs, and, increasingly, teachers need to know where to focus when the adrenaline kicks in. This is at least in part the reason for disaster drills: when the alarm sounds and the fear kicks in, they need to spring into action. First responders need to race to the scene, into the burning building, whatever, ready to save lives, when the normal instinct would be to run the other way. Fred Ryan, chief of police in Arlington, Massachusetts, describes how one of the most dreaded moments for him as a police officer is getting a call about a serious motor vehicle accident. "I don't want to go do this," he thinks. "But adrenaline kicks in. People are relying on your prompt response. You have to rise to the occasion."

The key to optimal performance in any endeavor is to practice. But practice isn't just about getting more comfortable with your speech or your slide deck or your lines; it's also about getting comfortable with playing your role. Practice is how most of us learn to do most things, and using power, like most things, gets easier—more natural, more skillful, and more automatic—the more you do it. It requires developing muscle memory and establishing routines for managing your attention, your mindset, and your physical (physiological) body.

Most people, when preparing for a big moment in the spotlight, focus mostly on what they are going to say. I've spent many a night tossing and turning, as words—some coherent, some not—march through my brain against my will before a big presentation. Trust me: it's not the most productive way to prepare. Much better, I've found, is to stand up, put on at least part of your costume (I usually wear my presentation shoes), handle your props (the laptop, the laser pointer, the slide advancer), and walk around while speaking. Let your body absorb and inform what you are trying to say; give it a chance to own the words.

Often, when coaching, I insist that the person I am working with actually practice the first thirty seconds of action that open the scene: enter the room or walk onstage, hold the mic, greet people individually on the way in, put down their things, pull out the chair and sit in it, or welcome others to a meeting. They learn to do things like taking their time to handle their props competently, to get settled into their chair before they begin speaking, practice what they are going to do with their hands so that they don't flail, and so on.

Rehearsal is a way of channeling nervous energy and avoiding some kinds of surprises, but also of conditioning yourself to expect a positive outcome, proving to yourself that you are perfectly capable of doing what you have to do and that you can handle whatever is coming.

In the science of optimal performance, peak performance is known as *flow*, which is basically the experience of losing yourself in time, space, and doing. Flow is the absence of self-consciousness. Flow is an aspirational state for an actor. And to achieve this state, you need to learn to manage where your attention goes.

Move off yourself. When acting with power, onstage and in life, it's the most natural thing in the world to be focused on ourselves, to feel exposed in the glare of the spotlight, to be hyperaware of the audience, and to imagine all of those eyes out there looking you up and down. Performance anxiety is, at its core, a self-conscious reaction. The only way to get on with the show in these moments is to lose your "self" in doing something. The key to owning the stage, owning the room, and owning the moment is to become absorbed in something, anything, besides how you look and feel.

Instead of being self-conscious, you can choose to be mindful of things outside yourself—that is, to focus so intently on something other than your internal self that there are no mental resources left for self-evaluation. This is probably the principle behind the old adage to imagine the audience in their underwear. In fact, mindful attention to the outside world is widely accepted as a useful approach to alleviating all kinds of anxiety. The idea is to learn to choose where your attention goes, and to practice doing something—feeling the breeze or listening to the fan in the room, or the sound of the ocean— that requires your full engagement.

When performing, instead of focusing on something distracting but irrelevant, you can choose to turn your attention on the other actors in the scene. This is what some actors do as an approach to handling stage fright, and I use a similar technique all the time. When I start to feel fearful, anxious, or worried about how I am going to perform, I shift my gaze onto the person I am dealing with and just focus on trying to take them in—it's like trying to listen with my eyes—and it absorbs all of my concentration. I observe carefully, and with curiosity, not judgment: "How is this person doing?" I ask myself. "What is going on for them?"

It also helps to remember that people aren't all that interested in you (or me) most of the time. Mostly, people are interested in themselves. We tend to overestimate how much others notice our actions and appearance; this bias in perception has been called the *spotlight effect*, and it happens all the time. When the news about me as "femme fatale" broke, a famous friend of mine reached out to share an incredible pearl of wisdom that I have repeated to friends in need many times. "The thing to remember," she said, "is that most people are mostly just thinking about themselves. They think about you for four seconds, and then they're back on themselves."

Embrace the fear. When Michael Powell was invited to join the Federal Communications Commission (FCC), he was just thirty-four years old. An army brat and the son of Colin Powell, Michael took his first job out of college as a cavalry platoon leader with the 3rd Squadron, 2nd Armored Cavalry Regiment in Amberg, Germany. At age twenty-four, he was badly injured in a training accident when he was ejected from a jeep that flipped and landed on him. He spent more than a year in recovery and then retired from the military. Powell worked briefly for the Department of Defense, went to law school, and then landed a position at the Department of Justice. When he got the call from President Bill Clinton offering him a seat on the commission, Powell was not expecting it. Nevertheless, as an ambitious, talented young man who was raised to value serving his country, it was an opportunity he couldn't refuse.

I met Powell one evening when we were both speakers at a program for Women in Cable Telecommunications, where I was giving a talk about stepping into power. At the end of the evening, he waited until the room had cleared before he approached me with a personal story. "When I was asked to join the FCC," he told me, "I was rattled. I felt I was too young, and that I wasn't qualified, and I really struggled with whether I should take the job." Finally, he admitted, his dad intervened. "He said, 'Son, you're just going to have to accept that sometimes other people know better than you do what you are capable of.'"

To hear Powell describe it, it was a classic case of performance anxiety. Surely he worried about doing something important with his life, playing an important role, and living up to his father's example; the former four-star general turned chairman of the Joint Chiefs of Staff had set a very high bar. At the same time, having been raised in a military family, he had always felt a responsibility to do something meaningful and strive to solve important social problems. "I grew up in a tradition of public service and leadership; I'm raised by a four-star general. It is a heavy responsibility when you are entrusted. You know, this position isn't for you, this is to serve the interests of the people of the U.S., it's a sacred and honorable tradition."

Ultimately, his desire "to serve," as he describes it, was greater than his fear. "I just embraced the fear," Powell said, when describing how he overcame the impulse to hide and found the courage to step into the role. "I was unafraid to admit that there was a lot I didn't know. I wanted to serve, and I wanted to excel, and to do that I knew I needed mentorship and guidance. . . . It was a great opportunity to learn, and all of these people became teachers and men-tors." Rather than feeling ashamed of what he didn't know, he became obsessive about learning. "I read like crazy," he recalls. "If you are prepared, I've learned, that is where your confidence comes from. And the more you do it, always, the more your confidence grows."

It wasn't the first time Powell felt unprepared for a job, and he says, "It hasn't been the last. It has become a principle of mine: when you have two choices, take the job that scares you. That's the one with the greatest potential to serve; the fear keeps you committed and focused and afraid of mediocrity."

Powell shows us how it's done. Within three years of his initial appointment, President George W. Bush appointed Powell as FCC chairman. And reservations aside, he burst onto the scene. Powell became a fierce advocate for consumer interests and made bold, sweeping changes that transformed the cable television industry and dramatically raised the profile of the FCC. Powell channeled his performance anxiety into action, and that enabled him to use the power of his role to achieve unprecedented impact.

Powell practiced great acting techniques without even knowing that was what he was doing. He embraced the fear and used it as motivation to give it his all. He saw the role as a duty, not an acco-lade or a verdict on his personhood. He viewed the power that came with a big role as an opportunity to solve other people's problems.

For Michael Powell, focusing on his responsibility to the country—instead of worrying about winning approval—kept his anxiety at bay. "I think it is important to have a point of view, to set out to do something. So many people I know just kind of nurse their job, are comfortable with not rocking the boat, making sure nothing goes wrong," he says. "Without a clear sense of purpose and direction, you are subject to every single person spinning you in circles; with no coherent agenda, you are just reacting and repelling. That was more scary to me than having an agenda. I knew what we were trying to do."

Powell's approach to playing his part demonstrates what David McClelland had in mind when he talked about how important it is for individuals who have a strong power motive to be equally driven by the need to achieve something beyond self-aggrandizement. It was exactly this balance—a high need for power coupled with a high need for achievement—that was associated in McClelland's research with effective performance in a high-power role.

Choose love. In a recent speech at Stanford, Oprah Winfrey said, "There's really only two emotions that count, and that's love and that's fear. And in all of your movements through life, you're either moving in the direction of one or the other. In order to have a meaningful life, you have to choose love." The same is true of acting with power.

As we have seen, performance anxiety heightens the need for approval and acceptance. But often we think the desire to be liked is the same as being likable. What really matters, of course, is how much *other* people think we like *them*. Dan Klein tells a story about how he figured this out, somewhat painfully, when he was teaching eighth-graders. "I really wanted them to like me," he says, but they sensed his fear that they wouldn't and played that power up, and for a short time, he struggled. One day, he thought about how he was playing his role and the objective he was coming in with. "I hope you like me" offers nothing to the recipient of that message. "I really like you," he found, worked much better.

To use power well, we need to show kindness, to offer acceptance and approval (when that makes sense), and to reassure others that we care about them, despite the fact that we are worried about ourselves. How do we do it? You can start by noticing which of your ambivalent feelings about performing is written all over your face. When we feel frightened, we tend to look serious, reserved, or aloof. When we are thinking of positive outcomes, we tend to look happy and friendly. A genuine smile can go a long way, which presumably was not lost on the legendary Harvard Business School professor Michael Porter, who used to write the word *Smile* in the upper right-hand corner of his first-day-of-class notes as a reminder to show up with love. Porter, a virtual celebrity in the business school world, understands that when you are in the spotlight, people watch your every move for clues about how you are feeling toward them.

When Bob Joss became the CEO of Westpac Banking Corporation, he was initially surprised to learn that employees were noticing his mood and his energy level when he passed them in the halls. If he was reserved or pensive, or just distracted, people thought he seemed aloof, that he didn't care about them or the firm, and they worried they had displeased him. So he started paying attention to these things—a friendly "hi" in the hallway, or how he took the stage. He worked on his energy and on trying to show his excitement and enthusiasm—he would kind of "hop up," he says, instead of walking. He felt he had to be "up" every day even when he didn't feel that way. And what he's learned about playing a big role, he says, is that "it is not important to act authentically, but it is very important to care authentically. If you really care, that will come through."

I love teaching. I love the interaction with students, who are mostly genuinely curious and eager to learn. And I love the excitement that comes from learning to see things in new ways. But I also dread the preparation and am always worrying about the person in the audience I don't know yet who may not like me or who might throw me off my game.

Early in my teaching career, I noticed that whenever I felt that something had not gone exactly my way in class, it was like a worm in my brain. I would ruminate endlessly, blow it way out of proportion, and find I couldn't make it go away. It was just that overwhelming sense that I had failed somehow, not been clear, forgotten to share something important, accidentally offended someone. I would obsess about that one student who seemed hostile, replaying the frowny face over and over, and wondering what else might be coming and how many other people were secretly turning on me. The fear took over, and it informed how I prepared to walk into class the next time. I was getting ready for a fight.

At some point, it occurred to me that my worry was not constructive. Not only was I out of touch with reality, I was actively cooling on the crowd at a time when it would have been much more productive to warm up toward them. I was filling my mind and my body with fear and anxiety: the precursors to hostility. And in teaching, on this dimension, you definitely reap what you sow.

I was not showing up open, generous, and eager to be with the students for eighty minutes, even though it should have been easy to do. What's worse, I was actively undermining my natural enthusiasm for something I genuinely loved doing. One day, out of desperation, when the frowny face showed up in my thoughts, I decided to think of a smiley face instead. It was a student who obviously loved the class and thought I was hilarious. Who asked great questions and shared when he was moved by something. It made me feel so much better, so I kept doing it—I would take a few minutes before each class to "think positive." I would replay great moments from previous sessions. I thought of the students who were most engaged, how they amazed me, and recalled instances of positive feedback. I thought of the times I got to witness a student having an "aha" moment. I tried to remind myself of those times when teaching and learning were most like playing.

I forced myself to think about the things that inspire me about teaching—what I love about it—rather than the things that drain me. It was a turning point in my life as an educator. It may not always come naturally, even to this day, but it is foolproof, and it is not hard to do. Choosing love over fear is one of many ways that an actor can be intentional about wanting to show warmth and caring in a powerful role and be truthful at the same time. There is nothing fake about it.

Stay present and connected. When feeling embarrassed, insecure, or powerless, connecting with your audience is key. After reading Patti Smith's essay about her experience with stage fright, I watched the video of the performance. At first, she stood still, almost motionless, as she sang: her eyes cast down, arms pinned to her sides, her mind clearly focused inwardly. Six minutes in, there was a break in the lyrics, a stanza on a steel-string guitar. With a bit of space, she heard the music. Her face softened as she looked up at the audience and, as if seeing them for the first time, she sang to them. She began to rock and sway, and she opened her arms, literally reaching out to the crowd as she sang. She was at one with her audience, at one with the music, and at one with the role she was playing. This inspired me, too.

In April 2016, six months after my "scandal" story broke, spring quarter started and I had to get back on the horse. There were 108 students assigned to my three sections and another 100-plus on the waiting lists. Some had undoubtedly read the news stories. I assumed they were not impressed. I did not know them, and they did not know me. What would they assume about my character? Plus, I didn't know who else might show up on the first day. Journalists had snuck in before. I was terrified.

This time, though, I knew what I needed to do. I had to stay focused on the students. Every minute, of every day, for nine weeks in that classroom, it had to be about them. Not about my desire to prove myself, to make them like me, or to get affirmation that I am a good person whom they might respect, but about tuning in to them and how they were doing, making sure they felt comfortable in a potentially awkward situation, and offering something that I hoped might be helpful or life-changing.

On the first day, I arrived early and stood at the lectern, waiting for them to arrive. But it made me feel alone. So I went and sat in one of their chairs. And when the first students came through the door I rose, moved toward them, and shook their hands as they filed in. It was a totally spontaneous reaction, but it felt so right. I shook every hand, met every student, locked eyes, heard their names, and tried to remember them. I gave them my undivided attention.

I have no idea what they were thinking or feeling in that moment. But to me, it felt, oddly, like having power.

PART IV

Understanding Abuses of Power, and How to Stop Them

7

When Power Corrupts
(and When It Doesn't)

Abuses of power make headlines. And, as a result, we know all too well what it means to use power badly. Whenever a person who is given power for the purpose of advancing group goals uses that power for selfish purposes—specifically, to advance personal goals at the expense of those in the group—it's fairly obvious that power is being abused. What is less obvious is when and why this happens and what the rest of us can do about it.

People seek power in many ways for many reasons, and this is not necessarily a bad thing. Studies show that a strong power motive is healthy and predicts effective leadership. But when people seek power as an end in itself, because they want to look, feel, and be more powerful, the results are entirely predictable. Wielding power without a real commitment to a role, or to solving other people's problems, predicts abuse and corruption of every imaginable kind.

The Root of All Evil

I've never met Dave McClure, but I admire his honesty. A self-proclaimed hillbilly from West Virginia who says he "barely graduated" from college and has been "geeking out" in Silicon Valley for more than twenty-five years, McClure has played big roles on a number of stages. In 2010, he co-founded the business accelerator 500 Startups to attract aspiring business owners who are not white, American, and male. McClure bet that by branding his firm as the go-to accelerator for female and international founders, who he believed were undervalued by the market because of social biases, he could capture the best overlooked talent. By July 1, 2017, the firm had more than $390 million in committed capital and had invested in more than 1,800 technology start-ups across the globe—fifty of those founders having successfully sold their companies for a profit, some in the hundreds of millions of dollars. And yet, on that very July day, McClure announced he was stepping down from his CEO role.

In the written statement announcing his resignation, McClure explained that he was handing over the company to his co-founder Christine Tsai after some "tough conversations" with senior management. The subject of those conversations was at that point widely known; on the previous day, McClure had been named among other high-powered men in a *New York Times* article reporting allegations of sexual misconduct in Silicon Valley.

At first, McClure had been defensive: "What did I do wrong?" But eventually he owned up to having repeatedly sexually propositioned a number of smart, high-potential businesswomen while they were trying to do business with him. "I made advances toward multiple women in work-related situations, where it was clearly inappropriate," he finally admitted. "I didn't have much empathy for the people I hurt and offended, and rather than face up to my own shallow motivations, I rationalized my actions and came up with reasons to find blame in others, rather than solely with me. . . . Somewhere, I had lost the plot."

To his credit, he owned it. But what explains this kind of thing? Why do people in positions of power lose track of the line between right and wrong? What drove McClure—someone who had founded and run a company with the explicit mission of helping female entrepreneurs gain power and opportunity—to change lanes?

These are age-old questions: Does power corrupt? If so, why? And what can the rest of us do about it?

My own research on the psychology of power provides some clues. In the lab, when we assign regular people to conditions in which they have power over others, or even prime them to think about having power, we find that they do lose the plot, in a sense. Without power on our minds, we navigate the social world carefully, trying to stay out of trouble, by engaging in what's called *self-regulation*. We track the plot, consider the context, and decide whether to pursue self-interest by considering the consequences for other people. But when power kicks in, our own objectives take over, and we are less inclined to consider anyone else's well-being or perspective.

Some people believe that power is the root of all evil, and that the abuse of power is a natural response to self-interest, embedded deep in our evolutionary code. This line of thinking suggests that powerful people act badly because they can, and that all of us, with power, would inevitably end up in this category. That all men, for example, are motivated by their sexual desires more than anything else, and would have sex at every opportunity, regardless of context, if they could.

This is Lord Acton's "power tends to corrupt" hypothesis, which implies that power turns all humans into the most profligate versions of themselves. And despite the abundance of examples out there, having spent the better part of my professional life reading, writing, studying, and teaching about these things, I don't buy it. Power does corrupt, sometimes, and these are the cases we hear about. But abuses of power are not inevitable. Power makes people more likely to act on whatever goals are most salient when the opportunity to use power arises.

The Effects of Power

Disinhibition. In 1998, between my first academic job at Northwestern and my arrival at Stanford, I spent a semester visiting psychologist Dacher Keltner at UC Berkeley, in search of a joint research project. It was the year of El Niño, and I was renting a garage apartment that flooded most mornings—to the point where I had to put on boots just to get out of bed. But no matter. It was one of the best times of my professional life. Our routine was to meet for lunch and walk to a local restaurant, where we tried to act relaxed and casual while groping for a good idea. One day, while we wrestled with giant burritos at a local Mexican place, Dacher shared a story about an experiment he had run in graduate school more than a decade earlier but never published.

Inspired by a famous faculty member who, apparently, ate his lunch with great abandon, he and his classmate Andrew Ward mischievously designed what is now known among researchers as "the cookie experiment." It was a test of the effects of power on manners and etiquette. University undergraduates were randomly assigned to groups of three and asked to discuss a long list of controversial university policy issues in sequence, and to write a group position statement on each one.

One of the three students in each group was then given a special role: to evaluate the other two by assigning them points based on their performance. But these points weren't simply a report card;

rather, they affected participants' chances of winning $400 in a lottery (points were like raffle tickets: the more you were assigned, the greater your odds of winning in a random draw). The person in this role of "judge," in other words, was given the power to control the others' outcomes.

Each group was videotaped as they huddled together, shared their opinions, and wrote position statements. About thirty minutes into the experiment, a lab assistant entered the room carrying a plate of cookies—four of them, to be exact—and offered them to the students. It was an intervention ingeniously designed to provide temptation on the one hand while invoking norms of etiquette on the other. Each of the three participants could safely take one cookie, but the remaining cookie posed a problem. It would be impolite to take the last cookie on the plate, knowing that there were no longer enough to go around. Using good manners would require consideration for one's coworkers, as well as self-control.

When the researchers counted who ate how many cookies, they found that across all groups, students assigned to the role of "judge" were more likely to help themselves to a second course. Having power, it seemed, had either increased their appetites or undermined their capacity to control them.

As soon as Dacher finished telling me his story, we knew we had found our research topic. In a flash of insight, this simple idea—power is disinhibiting—seemed to explain everything that we thought was interesting about power at the time. Since then, he and I—separately and together, with and without any number of others—have conducted many research studies and published many papers showing that when placed in positions of power or asked to think about being in a position of power, people act more readily on all kinds of impulses and approach all kinds of rewards that satisfy personal needs and desires, in ways that make the most sense to them, with less concern for the social consequences of their actions. For example, studies have found that participants assigned to high-power conditions rely more on stereotypes, are more likely to rearrange equipment in the lab to make themselves physically comfortable, are more creative because they are less influenced by precedent or others' ideas, and are more likely to express interest in working with an attractive but moderately competent work partner when primed to think of sex than those assigned to low-power conditions. So whether and how power corrupts depends on what goals are most pressing when the opportunity to use power presents itself.

Objectification. Abuses of power almost always involve the exploitation of other people. And when people have power, like McClure, they do treat others differently. We find that individuals who are granted power over others in the lab are more likely to view and treat those people as objects or instruments for achieving personal goals than as human beings whose own emotions and experiences matter.

McClure, like many in positions of power, at times used his role for personal gain instead of internalizing the responsibilities that came with it. He seemed to be "playing at" the role of investor, advisor, and mentor as a means of luring women into a context where he could (he felt) have his way with them. Sure, he hoped to accelerate business outcomes. But his actions reveal what was really going on for him. McClure was also on a quest for sexual validation. He had the money, he had control, and these women were eager to please him in ways that would not have been true in a different context. McClure held all of the cards, and still, he acted as though what he needed mattered most.

When disinhibition is coupled with insecurity about one's sexual prowess, subordinates are treated as sex objects and instruments of sexual validation. And when insecurity is primarily about social status, subordinates get treated like status symbols. It's as though what matters most about a subordinate—or a car, or a watch—is how that object reflects on the person who "owns" it.

One of the most heartbreaking examples I can think of is the college admissions scandal that broke in early 2019. Wealthy, powerful parents whose children were already advantaged by virtue of the many privileges that come with economic power were driven to bribe college administrators to gain admission for their children to specific high-status universities for which they may or may not have been qualified. Somehow, despite the fact that their children already had so many advantages in the college admissions process—paying for college was not an issue; some were coming out of well-known and respected college-prep schools; they had the means to receive tutoring to boost their GPAs, coaching in standardized testing, college essay-writing, athletics, or other extracurricular activities; and their parents were high-potential donors—the parents were so worried about where their children would or would not be admitted to college that they felt they had to cheat the system.

From the outside, it seems crazy: Why would these parents, whose children would have almost certainly earned admissions to a good college somewhere on their own, have risked so much to control the outcome of this process? My guess is that it came at least in part from fear of what would happen to their own status if their children failed to attend an "elite" university. Sadly, their kids became the objects, and the victims, of their parents' insecurities. Some of them didn't want to go to college at all; others did but have now been expelled and branded as cheaters. I'm sure these parents hoped to help their kids, not hurt them. But this is what happens when you have power, are insecure in your status, and use others—even those you love—to pursue a personal agenda without consideration of what it might cost them in the end.

Objectification takes different forms, depending on the power-holder's need. And studies of bullying and harassment show that when bosses feel powerless or deprived of influence and impact, things turn dark very quickly.

In 2017, I published a paper with Melissa Williams, now a professor at Emory, and Lucia Guillory, now a recruiting executive in Silicon Valley, on power and sexual aggression that memorably made this point. We asked both male and female participants ranging in age from late teens to late sixties about their long-term experiences with power and powerlessness (i.e., we asked them how powerless or powerful they felt in their lives). Two weeks later, we exposed them to a number of scenarios in which they were asked to imagine how they might respond to being rejected by a subordinate in whom they were sexually interested. Across the five studies we conducted, men and women who reported chronic feelings of powerlessness in their lives, when asked to imagine being in a position of power, reacted with more hostility toward a subordinate who rebuffed their advances. So although in previous work we found that power attracts people to useful targets, here we showed that power disinhibits aggression toward targets who don't make themselves useful. In some cases, people reported a greater willingness to make unwanted overtures toward an unwilling subordinate, and in others, they said they'd be more likely to retaliate professionally against the subordinate (e.g., by writing a bad letter of reference).

In one experiment, we created a task in which men assigned to either a supervisor or coworker role had the opportunity to send sexually suggestive messages to a woman online. The men were recruited using Amazon Mechanical Turk, ostensibly to participate in a study of how people remember information presented in online customer service platforms. The two parties met as avatars online and engaged in real-time chat messaging. When the male participants signed into the website where the study took place, they were paired with a female, whose young, attractive full-body avatar we designed ahead of time. Unbeknownst to the participants, the avatar was controlled by an experimental confederate; that is, she worked for us, so she knew what might happen, and no women were actually harassed in the experiment. Each male participant designed his own avatar and then sent messages (from a set we provided) for the woman to "learn." In each of twenty trials, each participant chose one message to send from a set of three message options we provided. In sixteen of the twenty message sets, there were two neutral message options and one sexually suggestive option (e.g., "What are you doing tonight besides me?"). In the four remaining trials, all of the options were neutral.

To us, the sexually suggestive messages seemed so forward and so outrageous we worried no one would send them. But we needn't have. On average, most of the men in our study sent at least one suggestive message, but overall, having power that day in the lab was not the reason. Those assigned to the supervisor role did not engage in more harassment than those assigned to play coworkers. Instead, it was male "supervisors" who reported being deprived of power in their lives outside the experiment who fired off more inappropriate and sexually charged text messages. And men who felt more powerful in general, outside the lab, were in fact slightly less likely to send harassing messages when assigned to the supervisor role. Having power, if anything, brought out their more responsible tendencies—as long as they felt they were already powerful in other ways to begin with.

Entitlement. Sometimes it seems that people in positions of power act as if they can do what they want, and that they deserve the things they want, just because they want them. Outside the lab, we see this entitlement narrative play out all around us: the very rich who don't pay taxes, the corrupt politicians who believe that they are above the law and that it's okay to stack the deck in their favor, media moguls who believe they have the right to have sex with any woman who enters their orbit.

One of my favorite (if much more benign) examples of this phenomenon is that extremely wealthy and otherwise impeccably mannered restaurant patrons sometimes order food that is not on the menu. They show up, sit down, and without looking at a menu tell the waiter in the most pleasant way, "I'd like a nice piece of fish tonight, grilled, with some fresh herbs, and is there any cantaloupe in the kitchen?" They don't acknowledge that they are going off script, even as the waiter hems and haws. It's as if the powerful customer has no awareness of context (at home, the chef makes whatever I want!) and therefore no capacity to adjust and play by the rules. Over time, people with power get so used to the advantages that come with it, they come to assume those advantages apply everywhere. This is what is happening when a powerful person can't get special treatment in a realm where they don't actually have power (like a restaurant, where the chef is in charge of what is for dinner, or at a place where money and status don't matter, like the DMV) and tries to insist, saying, "Do you know who I am?" These people are aware only of their desires in the moment, and assume that everyone else exists to cater to them, presumably because this is how things work in other parts of their lives. There is no attempt at perspective-taking, no acknowledgment that a wealthy person has no special status or power at the DMV, no self-control, no embarrassment or apology that might indicate recognition that their demands are out of bounds.

In the extreme, entitlement can lead powerful people to feel as though they "own" other, less powerful people, which means they have the right to control them by whatever means necessary. According to some experts, this way of thinking is what underlies the use of both emotional and physical violence in domestic abuse cases.

Lundy Bancroft, the author of *Why Does He Do That?* and an expert in abuse rehabilitation, believes that physical violence (usually by men) in domestic partnerships is less about a loss of control or disinhibition than a belief system that legitimizes the use of physical force and intimidation as perfectly acceptable means of controlling women (or spouses, romantic partners, and other family members) who "belong" to them. In domestic abuse, Bancroft argues, male abusers have learned—often from fathers who abused their mothers—that women are inferior to men, and that, like children, they are property, more like pets than partners, which entitles men to use their power to make "their" women behave. Violent outbursts are strategic in this view; they are part of a pattern of control-by-fear that is designed to frighten targets into submission. Of domestic abuse, Bancroft writes: "The roots are ownership, the trunk is entitlement, and the branches are control."

Villains, Victims, and Why It's Hard to Tell the Difference

Stories of victimization are highly subjective. This point was underscored by a viral video of Amaryllis Fox, a former CIA officer who spent ten years undercover investigating terrorism, on Al Jazeera talking about what she learned from her work. In the conflict between Americans and terrorist groups, she explains, we think they are the bad guys who want to kill us just because we are free. But Iraqis and Syrians, Fox learned in her time undercover, don't see it this way. In their minds, we are the bad guys—the wanton capitalist oppressors, waging war on Islam. From the point of view of al-Qaeda, she explains, they are Will Smith, and we are the extraterrestrial invaders. So often, in a contest for power, it is not always clear who is who.

Of course, there are power differences between victims and villains. But psychologically, it can be hard to tell the difference.

Many people who abuse power have been victimized themselves, often in the exact same ways. Psychologists tend to agree that when children are seriously deprived of parental affection, secure attachments, and a sense of themselves as capable, they grow up with heightened insecurities. And when they see an opportunity to get their needs met, they seize it. The same needs that lead us to seek power, to gain access to greater status, control, affection, and even sexual validation, tend to affect how we use the power we attain.

Three Types of Abusive Characters

Insecurities related to status, control, and sexual validation seem to go hand in hand—many people who abuse their power seem to be needy in all of these ways. Take the case of Steve Wynn—"the man who made Las Vegas." In February 2018, Steve Wynn resigned as chairman and CEO of Wynn Resorts on the back of accusations that he had harassed dozens of women—many of whom he allegedly coerced into sex—over the course of several decades.

Wynn is widely credited with having transformed the seedy and crime-riddled Las Vegas Strip into a tourist destination where anything can be bought and sold for people with money to burn. He built some of the most opulent hotel/casinos in the world, including the Mirage and the Bellagio, and reportedly brought the famous Siegfried & Roy act to town. Even after he fell off his pedestal and resigned, and his company's stock tumbled, his estimated worth still hovered around $3.5 billion.

An avid art collector with an outsized personality, Wynn ruled his casino empire with an iron fist and was reportedly known for screaming and banging his fists on the table during meetings, often while threatening to have people fired or removed. "I'm the most powerful man in Nevada," he'd yell, according to CNN and *The Las Vegas Business Review.*

But Wynn, unlike many other real estate moguls of his generation, was not raised in a gilded cage. His father, the son of a Lithuanian immigrant who changed the family name from Weinberg to Wynn when Steve was just six months old, owned and operated a chain of small-time bingo parlors. He traveled often to visit his parlors in upstate New York and Baltimore. But "something else kept him away from home, too: an addiction to gambling," wrote Nina Munk in a *Vanity Fair* profile. "Whenever Mike Wynn could find an excuse to extend a business trip, he'd land at the Tropicana, in Las Vegas, and hole up at the crap table, gambling away everything he had and then some." Mike Wynn died just as his son was graduating from college. So his son gave up his dream of going to Yale Law School to help run the bingo parlors and pay off the enormous debt (nearly $350,000) left behind by his father's gambling addiction.

Steve Wynn was like many who abuse their power: driven to do whatever it takes to manage their insecurities. Sometimes they act like bullies, other times like megalomaniacs, and often they are also sexual predators who use women and children to satisfy what often appears to be an extreme if not perverse need for some combination of affection, intimacy, dominance, and sexual gratification.

The Bully. A bully uses power to threaten and intimidate as a way of maintaining control. Often, a bully will claim this is necessary in order to hold people accountable. Research shows it is not.

When a person who controls our outcomes explodes in anger, acts snide, hurls insults, or offers "feedback" on aspects of our behavior that we cannot change, or at times when we cannot make a correction, the objective is not to be helpful or constructive, despite what those who rely on such tactics will tell you. Sometimes, it is to let off steam. Other times, it is to blame us for his failings. And often, it is to undermine our confidence; suggest that we are broken, unworthy, or pathetic; and make us feel dependent or indebted, and that we could not possibly find a better situation elsewhere.

This kind of "feedback" is a tactic, a power move, designed to shift insecurity from the source to the target. It is a way of trying to maintain power and control by disempowering the target psychologically. It is couched as "feedback" or "coaching," when in reality it is psychological warfare.

Here are some of the workplace bullying stories I have heard or witnessed just since I started writing this book. A boss tried to pit two subordinates against each other so that they wouldn't team up against him, by playing favorites, telling one she was special and the other that she could never do anything right, and refusing to meet with them, ever, in the same place at the same time. Another boss threw his shoe at a subordinate, a high-level executive, while she was eight months pregnant. When one subordinate asked her boss to refrain from discussing highly personal sexual topics while they were meeting, he called her a prude and said that if she couldn't find a way to get more comfortable with intimacy in her professional relationships, she would never make it in business. A bullying boss will justify his actions by saying they are necessary to achieve results. But now you know better.

To be clear, a bully is not the same thing as a tough boss. A bully uses power to maximize control as a means of elevating him- or herself, whereas a tough boss uses power to control group outcomes in a way that elevates others. A tough boss sets high but achievable standards and holds everyone accountable instead of singling individuals out for especially harsh treatment as a way of dividing the ranks. A tough boss gives recognition where it is due and accepts blame when it is warranted, instead of taking credit for others' achievements and blaming others for failures. And a tough boss is inclusive rather than divisive, and delivers feedback calmly and directly, instead of creating a scene in public, resorting to physical aggression, or trashing people behind their backs.

Negative feedback never feels good. But negative feedback from a tough boss is rarely emotionally overwhelming. When someone with power over you is unnecessarily critical, harsh, or demeaning; seems to enjoy criticizing you and not just your work; or goes out of his way to intimidate, embarrass, or threaten you, you are not dealing with a tough boss—you are dealing with a bully.

The Megalomaniac. The stories of how far some people will go to satisfy their need for respect, admiration, and power can be stranger than fiction—you can't make this stuff up. Elizabeth Holmes, the founder of Theranos, dropped out of Stanford as a freshman to build a biotech empire she claimed would revolutionize medicine. The technology, as it turns out, never worked, but she wasn't about to let that stop her. As John Carreyrou recounts in his bestselling book *Bad Blood,* Holmes berated employees who dared to question her and was quick to fire those who sensed that something was off. Dressed in Jobsian black turtlenecks and exuding a cold and exacting confidence, she drew scores of intelligent, experienced investors, board members, government regulators, and customers into her reality distortion field—they all wanted to be part of the next Apple—and after spending millions of other people's dollars on her vanity mission, she was finally indicted for fraud.

What explains this kind of behavior? Sometimes abuses of power are a response to needing to prove oneself worthy to people who are no longer there. A common story line is that of the celebrated leader who strives relentlessly to achieve greatness and prove himself worthy to a distant, absent, competitive, or abusive father. Those who choose fiercely competitive professional avenues—like entrepreneurship or politics—in which they can work independently and self-sufficiently, without having to take orders from others, often seem to fit this pattern. Elon Musk, Steve Jobs, Larry Ellison, Jeff Bezos, and Martha Stewart are all such cases.

Again, there is nothing inherently corrupt about pursuing power, or status, as a means of proving ourselves. In fact, studies—and the preceding examples—show that a high need for power is necessary (but not sufficient) for effective management, successful entrepreneurship, and even great leadership. It's when that need for power feels like a matter of life and death, such that nothing but power and status really matter, that it gets harder to play by the rules.

As any ambitious entrepreneur will tell you, when you are trying to change the world for the better, the ends justify the means. You do whatever it takes. Often, I hear entrepreneurs describe feeling like they are under attack and fighting for their lives when trying to build a new company. They feel they have to break down doors, refuse to take no for an answer, and squeeze the most out of everyone around them to keep their business alive and growing. This is how Dara Khosrowshahi, the former head of Expedia who replaced Travis Kalancik as Uber CEO, describes the culture he encountered there just after Kalancik was ousted. This kill-or-be-killed mentality "was the right thing for the business in the beginning, it was necessary," he says. "And it led to all of the other problems that ended up getting Kalancik fired."

To a megalomaniac, every social interaction is an opportunity to seize power, claim status, and remind others how important, how needed, and how special one is. Relationships with a megalomaniac that do not serve this purpose do not work. A megalomaniac cannot accept defeat or even own a mistake. A megalomaniac takes credit for every success and blames others for every failure. A megalomaniac feels entitled to privileges that are not her right. This kind of person must be at the center of things and must orchestrate contexts in such a way that if she leaves, the effort cannot continue.

The Don Juan. The type of behavior exhibited by Steve Wynn—a high level of sexual activity and difficulties with commitment and intimacy—is known among power researchers as *Don Juan syndrome*. But contrary to what that moniker implies (and what many people believe), chronic sexual misconduct and promiscuity among powerful men is not evidence of how "cocky" or self-assured these men are. It is actually better understood as an expression of desperate insecurity or pent-up frustration that seeks relief when power presents opportunities.

Sometimes, when power leads to sexual misconduct, it is because it is lonely at the top. Male power-holders who fear they are unlovable, according to some psychologists, seek love from every woman they meet. Power can also make people paranoid about the reasons that people are near them, and this heightens the need to test whether others really, truly love them. Other times, when power leads to sexual misconduct, it is because of another kind of insecurity. Social scientists use the term *precarious masculinity* to describe the social pressures, in a male-dominated world, of needing to constantly test and prove one's masculine power. In the same way that power and aggression are linked when the reason for using power is to preserve a position of social dominance and superior status, power and sex are linked when the reason for using power is to achieve dominance and validation of a different kind.

In June 2011, Anthony Weiner—the brash and argumentative congressman from New York—was caught, literally, with his pants down. Using a bizarre pseudonym—Carlos Danger—he had texted a revealing, close-up selfie showing just his underwear to a woman he barely knew. Unsurprisingly, the scandal quickly made national news. No one could understand why this ambitious and talented politician—who had handily won seven terms by over 60 percent of the vote—would so carelessly jeopardize his bright and promising future by sending such a photo. One incredulous New Yorker—

Barbara from Bell Harbor—called in to *The Brian Lehrer Show* on WNYC, her local NPR station, and left a voicemail asking, "What is going on with these people? I would love to see a psychological study of what kinds of people are always unzipping their pants." Lehrer needed an expert to shed some light on the situation. So his producers called me.

The segment was called "Why Do Politicians Behave Badly?" and I was asked to explain what leads political leaders to engage in sexual misconduct with such regularity. I emphasized what I knew at the time: *We all have needs and insecurities*, I said, *but in positions of power people act on them.*

However, since then I've learned some things and have come to a more nuanced understanding of the interplay between sex and power, at least in men. The needs for power and sexual validation have an underlying motivation in common. Feeling painfully insecure—unlovable, undesirable, weak, incapable, or unimportant— drives the desire for both power and sexual validation. So although having power does not make all men more sexual, in some men, the concepts of power and sex have an automatic association, such that thoughts of one concept automatically activate thoughts of the other. In these kinds of men, having power creates opportunities to fulfill sexual needs, and having sex is a way of fulfilling the need to feel powerful. And some evidence suggests that these kinds of men gravitate toward powerful roles more than others. A high need for power, when unbalanced by other, more socialized motives (like the need for achievement or belonging), predicts holding powerful positions, but is also associated with high levels of sexual activity (including various kinds of misconduct) and a lack of impulse control.

When President Clinton had an affair with a White House intern, it almost cost him his job. At first he denied it, but he was forced to own up. It was not the first time, we learned, that he had strayed from his marriage. Hillary Clinton stood by him, she never flinched, and she caught some flak for it. But later, in an interview, she explained her stance toward her husband. "He was abused," she said, calling his mother "a doozy." Without going into much detail, she described how his mother had abandoned him, left him in the care of a grandmother who despised her, and then returned to fight the grandmother for his affections. "When a mother does what she did," said Hillary Clinton, "you keep looking in all the wrong places for the parent who abused you."

The needs for love, intimacy, secure attachment, and belonging are among the most fundamental drivers of human psychosocial development. And secure attachments to one's primary caregivers in childhood are a cornerstone of psychological health and a basis of developmental maturity. Secure attachments help us internalize the belief that we are lovable. They make it possible to trust others implicitly, to be comfortable with intimacy and vulnerability, to make commitments, and to put others first. Because parenting is imperfect by definition, most—maybe all—of us come into adulthood with questions about whether we are lovable enough. And when the needs for affiliation, intimacy, love, and sexual validation are chronically elevated, power presents opportunities that can be very hard to resist.

For those seeking this kind of validation, others' expressions of reverence, adoration, and the desire to please can also be intoxicating. This is why some men find vulnerability and submissiveness in others arousing. Arousal isn't inherently sexual, although it can sound that way. *Arousal* is a general term for a physiological response to stimulation of any kind. In fact, arousal can become sexualized by accident. Classic studies by Stanley Schachter, for example, showed that when people are physiologically aroused because they've been pedaling a stationary bicycle, or are anticipating receiving a shock, they can easily misattribute their feelings. And in some circumstances, the fear associated with an unpleasant event attracts people to one another as well.

In one famous study by psychologists Donald Dutton and Arthur Aron, male passersby crossed a suspension bridge on foot in Vancouver, British Columbia, and were met on the far side by a female experimenter. Some crossed a shaky bridge, while others crossed a stable one. The experimenter approached prospective participants as they stepped off the bridge with a short questionnaire that asked them to write a brief story about a sketch showing a woman covering her face with one hand and reaching out with the other. Afterward, the experimenter thanked the respondent, wrote her phone number on a corner of one of the questionnaire pages, tore it off, and handed it to the participant, explaining that she would be happy to explain the experiment in more detail when she had more time. Men who had crossed the shaky bridge attributed their physical arousal to sexual feelings: they wrote stories that contained more sexual content, they reported feeling more attracted to the experimenter, and they were more likely to call her later and ask her out.

These studies show that sexual attraction is not always what it appears, and the same is true of sexual harassment. We tend to think of sexual attraction, sexual compulsiveness, and sexual aggression as expressions of powerful feelings, but in fact, all can be reactions to the kinds of generalized physiological arousal that accompany anxiety, stress, and fear.

The sexual harassers we are reading about these days do not look like self-satisfied, happy-go-lucky, or opportunistic playboys who were just enjoying the scenery. Many of them were compulsive. Some had fetishes. They were calculated, sociopathic even, in their exploitation of professionally hopeful, unsuspecting young women in situations from which it seemed there was only one way out. They manipulated, threatened, and sometimes drugged or physically forced themselves on women who were not sexually interested in them. These are not the actions of people who feel powerful. These are the actions of people who feel desperate.

8

How to Wrangle a Bully

Alternatives to Playing the Victim

M ost of us have to deal with a bully in one shape or form at one time or another. Sometimes a bully seems to come out of nowhere—this happens online, where certain kinds of people seem to be lying in wait, just looking for opportunities to land a punch. And often a bully will kind of sneak up on you. First he'll win your trust, and you will give him power by offering rights, respect, and a big part in your story. And eventually he will turn that power against you in ways you did not see coming. It could be a boss, a mentor or coach, a beloved parent or sibling, a friend to whom you feel indebted and have pledged loyalty, or a partner you promised to love, honor, and cherish whatever the cost.

If you have been bullied, you know how it feels to be terrorized and disempowered by someone else's surprisingly aggressive attempts to control you. A bully makes you feel like a powerless victim. But being victimized by a bully does not mean you have to play the victim role. Playing the victim is accepting a bully's version of reality, behaving as though he has the right to hurt you, and believing your only option is to try to get back on his good side.

So far, the message of acting with power has been to take responsibility for making others feel secure. But this assumes a cooperative world in which we want our relationships to work. When it comes to dealing with someone who abuses their power at your expense or takes advantage of your deference and generosity, you may need to change tactics. You want to do no harm, but take no crap. Sometimes, when a person hands you more than your share of it, you can learn to say, "No thanks. I think this belongs to you," and hand it back.

When we are in the thick of things, it is hard to see the alternatives. But as anyone who has survived bullying knows, it is possible to take back your life. It is possible to act in ways that shift the balance of power.

In large part, wrangling a bully is an exercise in reclaiming your story and control of the plot, reimagining your role, and finding the courage and discipline to try a new way of acting. There are things you can do to stop the abuse, disarm the bully, detach from the megalomaniac, or escape any other kind of psychological predator, no matter how helpless you feel. The key is to approach the drama in a way that deprives the flames of oxygen, instead of inadvertently feeding them.

The first step is realizing that although you feel trapped, you always have choices. No one has the right to control you—we choose to give others that right, and we can choose to take it away. No one has the right to define who you are, to force you into an undesirable role, or to dictate how you must behave to avoid further aggression. No one has the right to drive all of the plot twists, to create incessant drama, to insist that your story is wrong, or to hurt you while insisting they are acting out of love and caring. Your story belongs to you. And although it doesn't always feel that way, we all have the power to reclaim authorship of our own story lines, to trust our own instincts, and to choose how we use the power we have to respond to the bad actors who enter our realm.

Tom was in his midforties, a talented professional mediator working for a private financial services consulting firm. Tom was highly skilled, with twenty years of experience, and he was known for being diplomatic, easygoing, and polite. His clients took to him easily.

His boss, on the other hand, was all over Tom's case. Everything about Tom seemed to bother him. To start, there was his accent. Though it was barely perceptible to most people, before he got on the phone with clients his boss would sometimes ask, "Could you not use that accent you use?"

Then there was the way he dressed. The company had a "business casual" dress code, which explicitly stated that employees need not wear suits unless otherwise directed. One day, as Tom headed into a meeting wearing dress pants, a French cuff shirt, and a brand-new sports coat, his boss cornered him: "Why aren't you wearing a suit?" Another time, Tom was scolded for wearing his sunglasses—not in a meeting, but in the lobby of the building. And on yet another occasion, his boss dressed him down for checking his luggage on a business trip they took together because it meant the boss would have to wait while Tom collected his bags. Tom tried to be accommodating. Each time his boss berated him he would apologize and promise to do better next time. But after eighteen months he had reached his limit. Tom walked out the door and never came back.

Exit, stage left. This is one way to stop abuse, by taking control of the ending. Tom had power too, and he did not need to stick it out or make it work. Of course, not everyone in these kinds of situations can just quit or walk out the door. But most of us do have power in a relationship with a bully, even when that person makes us feel as if we don't. In most cases, we have more control over what others are able to do to us than we think.

One of the reasons that cycles of abuse tend to feel inescapable is that victims of abuse learn to behave as though they are helpless even when they are not. The first studies of learned helplessness showed that animals who received shocks but did not learn to control them eventually gave up and stopped trying to avoid the pain. But animals who learned that pressing a lever would stop the shock continued to fight to protect themselves and to avoid repeating painful experiences. More recent research on post-traumatic stress disorder supports the same conclusion: when a victim is able to take action in the midst of a crisis—to crawl out of the car in an accident or to rescue someone else—the impact of the trauma is less devastating, less disempowering, psychologically. The way out is to focus on acting, on doing something, to save yourself. You have to press the lever. Like so many of the other challenges we have addressed in this book, when it comes to stepping out of the victim role, the first step is to act differently.

Fatal Attractions

A great irony in all of this is that people who abuse power are often extremely seductive. Why are we drawn to these people? Why do we fall in love with them? Idolize and want to work for them? Or vote for political candidates who spew hate (even toward us)? We are drawn to these kinds of people, especially when we feel powerless, because their strength, fortitude, and success at controlling others makes us feel secure in their presence, whether they have any intention of protecting us or not.

Let's start with the reality that—as Henry Kissinger opined—power is the ultimate aphrodisiac. According to evolutionary models, we are attracted to high-power mates because as partners, they increase our own odds of successful procreation and survival. And we see this reflected in our culture: power of all kinds predicts sexual

attractiveness, and vice versa. Having power makes potential partners more attractive, and physical attractiveness is a source of power.
In a recent study of online dating profiles, for example, UC Berkeley
psychologist Dana Carney and her colleagues analyzed dating profile photos and found that (regardless of gender) the more dominant (i.e., physically expansive) a person appears, the more potential
dates expressed interest by swiping right.

Evolutionary forces aside, power is also seductive simply because
a powerful partner is like a trophy—it's a sign of your own status and
value to the rest of the world. And knowing that someone who could
have anyone has chosen you isn't hard on the ego either. For most of
us, it's thrilling—and a little bit scary—to be in the presence of a powerful person. This is one reason why women are drawn to aggressive
men, and underlings are sometimes eager to accept invitations to
drinks, or dinner, or travel, for example, for reasons that have nothing to do with interest in sex per se and everything to do with prox-
imity to power.

People often joke about women with "daddy issues," but the
truth is often quite sobering. In some pockets of the political science
community, it is believed that voters (of both sexes) relate to political figures as parental surrogates and often prefer the "strong father" type. This type of leader is especially appealing to those who
feel they need protection and who feel safer with a "tough parent" in
charge. This dynamic could explain the high numbers of women
voters who have historically supported President Trump, for example, despite his antifeminist positions.

This might also shed light on why the most vulnerable groups
and individuals are often the first to flock to such a leader, and why
it is so easy for leaders to exploit those groups' fears, insecurities,
and feelings of powerlessness (as Trump did in courting the struggling white working class). It may also explain why a number of

Trump's most high-profile followers—like Cesar Sayoc, the socially reclusive ex-stripper turned pizza deliveryman who sent pipe bombs through the mail to a long list of the president's political enemies—have referred to the president explicitly as the father they never had.

This is also why, tragically, victims of abuse who were deprived of love, attention, and kindness as children sometimes end up leaving one type of abusive relationship for another. Growing up with a bully makes people feel unlovable, and at the same time it teaches the lesson that abuse is an expression of love. For example, women who have been mistreated or neglected by their fathers, in particular, can be especially prone to falling in love with abusive men, whose form of showing love feels familiar. Familiar dramas make it easy to play the parts we know best. Daughters may be drawn to romantic partners who bully them because of how their fathers treated them, but they also learn to play the victim role from watching their mothers—if mothers put up with mistreatment, if they excuse it or try to share the blame, this defines for daughters what is acceptable, and what it means to be a good woman. And this is how old, unhealthy patterns get perpetuated. But according to experts, it is not how the story has to end. By stepping outside ourselves and looking at the whole picture—as a playwright might—we can start to identify opportunities for changing the plot, rewriting old scripts, "killing off" tired characters, and reimagining the ending.

Stay Out of the Crosshairs

The experts will tell you that the best way to avoid being bullied is to avoid getting involved with a bully. Well, duh. But it is not always easy to recognize a wolf in sheep's clothing. Perhaps the most important thing any of us can do is to learn to know a powermonger when we see one. Maya Angelou famously warned, "When someone shows you who they are, believe them the first time." The ability to recognize the signs that someone is looking for a victim is a critical skill.

Know the red flags. For starters, watch out for someone who doesn't take no for an answer. Often, this starts sweetly, and it can be flattering to be pursued, for a while, even against our will. But someone who acts as though your preferences don't matter is telling you he does not care about what you want. Framed another way, this kind of aggressive pursuit can be a veiled sign of disrespect. If someone comes on too strong and does not seem to take your preferences seriously, embrace the fear; trust your first instincts and keep your distance.

Powerful actors can make us feel as though we are under a spell. But feeling incapable of acting with volition in someone else's presence is never a good sign either. People who abuse power tend to have an extreme need for control and, as such, are often charismatic (as well as scary)—they have a finely honed ability to draw others in, to charm, seduce, and manipulate. At the same time, they are also hypercritical, and have an extreme need to be the most important person in every room. Watch out for people who treat you as though you are very special while at the same time showing disrespect or contempt for almost everyone else. They are trying to solidify their control over you. Sooner or later, when you can't fulfill their insatiable needs for power, control, and obedience, they will demote and demean you, too.

Sheryl Sandberg is known for her advice that women avoid the "cool" guys when seeking a romantic partner and, instead, learn to value the nerd. This is a power story in and of itself. It can feel empowering to "win" the attention of that person—whether it's a romantic partner, a friend, or a boss—who can choose anyone in the world and who makes you feel as though you are the only person

worthy of their affections. But choosing this type of partner minimizes your power, your rights, and your ability to get what you need
and deserve from your relationships. Learn to recognize who makes
you feel safe, not just spellbound.

Don't take the bait. If you can't create physical distance between
yourself and a bully, you can maintain psychological distance by refusing to engage with bad behavior. People who abuse power crave
evidence that they are powerful, that what they do has an effect.
They will do everything possible to keep you on your toes. If you
take the bait by showing that you are fearful, angry, or even apolo-
getic, you are making it fun for them.

Kids often receive this advice for dealing with a schoolyard bully,
and it works with adults the same way. A person with an elevated
need to dominate needs not only to play the dominant role but also
to have that position validated again and again by others who play
the helpless, compliant victim. Status contests are fun for some people, and they will do whatever they can to first lift you up and then
tear you down. Any suggestion that you are hurt or angered by this
will make the game exciting. So the goal (this may be the only time
you ever receive this advice) is to be *as boring as possible*. It is not the
same as pretending whatever happens is okay by smiling or playing
along. It is more like simply missing your cue, showing disinterest, or
even just appearing bored, acting like nothing happened. As we have
already seen, acting inattentive or disinterested is unfriendly, and
this part is important. It indicates that you do not want to play,
and that if pushed, you will not make it fun. More often than not, the
bully will eventually look for a more satisfying target.

Know, but don't blame, yourself. Victims of abuse often blame
themselves for the pain they endure. In part, this is by design; accusing a victim of causing the abuse is one of many ways that a bully

maintains control. Often, it feels too dangerous to blame the people who hurt us because we feel dependent on them. For example, victims of child abuse are often unable to confront their abusers because of how much they need their parents. Employees who are victims of harassment at work often tolerate abuse because they fear retaliation and losing their jobs. When you can't assign blame to the person causing harm, you assume you did something to deserve the abuse, and you punish yourself with shame, self-loathing, and all kinds of self-destructive behaviors. You can't always blame or punish your aggressor, but when you blame yourself for others' transgressions against you, they win.

Women who are bullied by their romantic partners commonly come to believe there is something wrong with them, that if only they were prettier, sexier, more attentive, and so on, they might be treated with the care they deserve. They side with their tormentors, beat up on themselves, and continue to carry out their abusers' dirty work for them. In order for abuse victims to move past the psychological effects of the trauma, they must learn to see abuse for what it is and accept that they are not at fault for what has happened to them. And of course, they must learn safe ways to fight back.

Don't act like a victim. As we've learned, if you have been abused by someone with power, you have, unfortunately, been in training. You know how to have a relationship with someone who abuses their power, and it probably feels familiar. So you may be drawn in again. But not only that: people who have been exploited before often appear exploitable. They wave green flags without knowing it—"Look over here! I can tolerate anything!"—by advertising how humble and accepting they are, how hard it is for them to say no, how readily they blame themselves for everything, and how eager they are to please. Bullies are drawn to those who send these kinds of signals. One of the most important things any of us can do is to become aware of factors that make us a target. Again, this is not about changing who you are, it is about developing ways to protect yourself by choosing which sides of yourself to advertise, to whom, and which to conceal.

When it comes to explaining who becomes a target of abuse and why, many myths abound. For example, in contrast to the convenient fiction that women who are sexually abused were "asking for it" by acting flirtatious, appearing attractive, or dressing provocatively, some studies show that the opposite is more often true. Rape and sexual assault are so common in our society that it is hard to even identify target trends, and for sure, whenever anyone is raped the perpetrator is to blame. But some studies of stranger rape find that victims are more often dressed in conservative clothing with arms and legs covered than in provocative attention-grabbing attire. Research finds that the victims of stranger rape are also no more attractive on average than women who are not targets.

Studies of criminal behavior reveal what an attacker looks for in a victim: a person who looks easy to take down. Victims of street crimes are not necessarily smaller or physically weaker than others. They just act differently: more submissively, without clear direction or purpose, and without paying much attention to their surroundings. This, not their size or stature, is what makes them seem easy to overpower.

Luckily, as we have seen already, it's not that hard to adjust the ways we carry ourselves, and many of us learn this naturally as we adjust to living in environments in which crime is common. When I moved to Manhattan after spending most of my life in a small college town, for example, I vividly recall learning that no matter how lost I was in the city, I had to move like I knew where I was going. I would come up out of an unfamiliar subway, and instead of standing on the corner, looking up at street signs, and trying to get oriented, I would charge forward, keeping pace with the flow of foot traffic as though I knew where I was headed. If I learned I was walking the wrong way, I would stride confidently to the next corner, cross the street, and double back on the other side.

When it comes to verbal or emotional attacks, carrying yourself with direction and purpose will also, in most situations, make you a less appealing target. It helps to have clear boundaries, clear priorities, and determination. Or, at least, to act as though you have these things.

Choose contexts carefully. As we have seen already, what gives someone power is not just who they are and what resources they control but also the contexts in which they operate. When I lived in New York I was never victimized on the street. But when I lived in Chicago I was once robbed at gunpoint. I was with two friends—one a tall, strapping man—and it had just turned dark. Later, as we talked with police, they pointed out that although the block was well lit, there was one streetlight out, directly over the spot where we were accosted. This was not a coincidence. Criminal behavior is most likely to occur in places where no one else can see it happening.

I am very careful about this now, and I advise many of the young women I work with to stay out of the shadows, not just on the street, but at work. No meetings in private places outside the office, at night, or in someone's car. And avoid the walk-and-talk. Dinners outside of the office can also be hazardous, I've learned, depending on where you sit. It is not uncommon, apparently, for female PhD students, job candidates, and assistant professors to be groped at a work dinner under the table while sitting next to a senior male colleague.

The norms that define what is professional or acceptable after work hours, outside of the office, are much looser, so what counts as out-of-bounds is much more equivocal. Anytime you are meeting outside a work space, you are no longer really in public because no one knows you or the nature of your relationship, and the line between acceptable and inappropriate behavior becomes less clear. When someone looks you up and down and comments on how attractive you are in a meeting room, for example, it feels out of line right away. But when you show up at a work party after hours, or at a bar, commenting on your appearance can seem more "normal," or at least within the bounds of acceptable behavior, making it harder for you to trust your internal signals about what is appropriate or not.

Similarly, I have heard more than once about bosses who flat-out refuse to meet in an office, and then use a walk-and-talk to deliver emotional abuse. Walking around not only lowers the chances that anyone will overhear or witness what is happening, it also makes social boundaries unclear. It is one thing to stand and excuse yourself from a meeting; it is another to suddenly veer off in a different direction while your boss is supposedly leading the way. And a harsh or inappropriate remark is much easier for the boss to pass off or dismiss as a meaningless comment made casually on the fly than one that is made in a formal setting, like a meeting or in someone's office. Context matters in all of these ways. So a good strategy to protect yourself from bullying is to stay out of a context that is too private, or one in which the norms and roles that define appropriate behavior are murky.

Police the border. In addition to being diligent about physical contexts, it is also important to police your emotional boundaries. In today's workplace, where many employees are expected to be "on call" at all hours, violation of work-life boundaries is a common offense. Many of the victims I talk with are terrified of pushing back on those who seek to exploit them with unreasonable requests. I advise them to say no firmly, and with a big smile. Everyone needs a nice way to say no—"Sorry! Can't help you. Good luck!" Or, as my teenagers have been known to say, with a laugh, "That sounds like a 'you' problem." You might not want to say this aloud to your boss, but you can certainly think it, and it might help you appear less compliant and avoid saying "yes" when you shouldn't.

A friendly but firm *no* is like advertising that your home has a security system. Most criminals—and most bullies—will keep looking for an easier target.

Research on prisoners' dilemma games finds that being unconditionally cooperative in a competitive situation invites exploitation, and studies of bullying reinforce this conclusion. In schools and workplaces, bullies target individuals who they think will not fight back: people who are nice to everyone all the time and who seem to tolerate things that others won't. Social isolation is also a risk factor, in part because bullies target individuals who are unlikely to appear with witnesses in tow or to have allies who are willing to protect them.

Whether you are alone or not, the key is to know where your boundaries are, to learn to recognize when they have been crossed, and to have simple go-to ways of reinforcing them. You can be friendly and cooperative as long as others are doing the same, but if someone crosses a line, you can react by simply noticing. It helps to do so immediately and to have a zero-tolerance policy.

Check it out. Inappropriate behavior of all kinds persists when it is tolerated. No one wants to make a federal case out of every transgression, and research on nonverbal behavior suggests that this is actually unnecessary and not even likely to be effective. Rather than becoming emotional or making a big speech, it can be more powerful to just notice by staring, without smiling. If someone puts their hand on your leg, just look at their hand for moment, then shift your eyes to their face and don't look away until you can see it is registering. If it doesn't, just carefully move their hand off your body. If someone says something inappropriate, just stare a little longer than usual. Simply noticing puts a perpetrator "on notice" and begs a justification. It is a way of making it clear that what you witnessed is not normal and of silently insisting on an answer to the question, *Why did you just do that?*

I'm asked often how to deal with workplace bullies who ignore, interrupt, and talk over others; who demean others with insulting comments and jokes; who yell and throw tantrums. The most common responses to being interrupted while speaking are to either stop talking or raise one's voice. Neither of these is particularly effective. Raising one's voice, in particular, can sound shrill and communicate fear and defensiveness, which often only excites those who are trying to stir things up. Far better is to firmly raise a finger to signal *stop* or *wait,* or to say simply, "I'm almost done." Raising a finger—pointing—as I've already observed, is surprisingly powerful. Just moving the arms away from the body seems to indicate a willingness to fight back, and that finger seems to work like a weapon. Nonverbal gestures are often more effective than verbal contests, particularly for women. In fact, one recent study by Emory University's Melissa Williams and Scripps College president Larissa Tiedens found that while verbal assertiveness or dominance can provoke backlash for women, nonverbal assertiveness does not.

It takes tremendous discipline to resist being triggered emotionally by someone who appears angry or in a rage. Many people report responses such as shutting down, tearing up, shouting back, trying to defend themselves, and simply fleeing the scene. But generally, the better move is to calmly notice and refuse to engage. I have used this technique many times when I don't like how things are going. I've said things like "You know what? I don't like the turn this has taken, so I'm going to leave now," or "I can see you are really upset about this, so let's talk later." No matter how much power the person has, it is perfectly appropriate to excuse yourself and end a meeting in which you feel unsafe. Exit, stage left.

One executive I know reports that instead of getting flustered or defensive when a particularly intimidating board member barks out insulting comments, he simply asks, "What do you mean by that?" I've also witnessed someone shut down a veiled threat by looking the perpetrator straight in the eye and asking, "Did you really just say that?" Phrasing your rebuke as a question is more effective than scolding, at least in part because it pushes the burden of explanation onto the perpetrator. Stormy Daniels, the adult film star who has famously managed to force President Trump to explain the payoffs she received to keep quiet about their affair, is a master of this technique. In an interview with *60 Minutes* she explained how she dealt with Trump's tendency to drone on about himself and his accomplishments. Daniels would ask, "Does just talking about yourself normally work for you?" By calmly turning the spotlight onto the other person's bad behavior, we can shift the balance of power.

Grin and bare teeth. In 2017, Canadian prime minister Justin Trudeau played his power up while meeting President Trump for the first time at the White House. Presumably, he had noticed (as many journalists had) that Trump used a special handshake when meeting other heads of state. As dignitaries approached him at a polite distance, he would lean in toward them with his arm outstretched, grab them by the hand, and then yank them forward so that they would lose their balance and stumble toward him. Presumably, he felt that taking control physically gave him the upper hand psychologically. But when Trudeau emerged from his car that day, he effectively neutralized Trump's signature hand-yank by rushing in to meet him at close range, clutching Trump's right hand in a firm shake, pawing Trump's right shoulder with his left hand, and smiling widely, but with his jaw clenched. It showed zero polite hesitation and an absence of caution; it also showed that he was not afraid, that he was not going to let Trump set the tone, and that he would not be intimidated—that Trump had met his match.

When facing a dominant actor, it is natural to defer. It can be frightening to try to win a power contest with this kind of person, who makes it seem there is no line they won't cross. But at least sometimes, when an actor plays power up, it's good to play it up more. It helps to think about what exactly you are afraid of. Remember that bullies are often acting aggressively because they feel weak. And that means that sometimes it pays to call their bluff.

I recently coached two female executives about how to handle an abusive boss who was playing them off against each other—treating one as the favorite child and verbally demeaning the other. They had put their heads together and figured out what was going on. Now they wanted a way to stop it. Neither of them wanted a confrontation; they were scared of offending the boss and losing their jobs (or worse). So we devised an acting-with-power approach: when you meet, be friendly—business as usual—but look him in the eye and recite a simple, silent mantra to yourself as often as needed: "I know what you're up to." We practiced it on each other and were delighted by how subversive it felt and how scary we appeared while doing it. People like their boss need validation that they are fearsome; they need acquiescence, appeasement, and trepidation. This subtle approach was designed to offer none of these rewards and to put him on notice—*we know what you are up to and we are devising a counterattack*—in hopes that he would turn his energies toward something more satisfying. It didn't take long, they tell me. When it stopped being fun for him, he stopped playing his game.

Show empathy. I know, this sounds strange. But sometimes it is possible to stop bullying by acting to convey understanding. Hostage negotiators describe *active listening*—a form of dialogue that involves recognizing the other person's perspective, asking open-ended questions, and demonstrating genuine interest, among other things—as the only way to disarm a desperate person with a gun or a bomb, and the same principle holds here. Showing empathy is not the same as siding with or excusing the perpetrator. It is showing deference strategically to protect yourself and others. Conflict resolution experts explain that the motivation to defend one's honor is at the root of many kinds of violence. So alleviating shame by showing compassion and understanding, even forgiveness, toward someone who is contemplating or has already taken violent action is widely practiced by experts and often touted as an effective approach for talking someone out of escalating and doing more damage.

No matter how much or how little power we might have, acting with human understanding and showing we care about our enemy's suffering is something any of us can offer, with no cost to ourselves.

The Bystander Role
and New Ways to Play It

How to Stop Bad Actors
from Stealing the Show

S nackman is an unlikely name for a superhero, but in the eyes of many, that is what he was. For Charles Sonder, a twenty-four-year-old architect living in Brooklyn, New York, a Thursday evening in March 2012, began like any other as he left one bar around 9:30 and hopped the subway to meet friends at another. To sustain him on his journey, he had purchased a can of Cheddar Pringles and a bag of gummy bears, and was contentedly snacking away. Suddenly, at the Spring Street station, a stranger rushed in just ahead of the train's closing doors and sent a female passenger into a rage. She was shouting at, hitting, and kicking him, and he began to fight back. It was quite a spectacle, and naturally one passenger whipped out his cellphone to capture the action.

The footage shows each party landing a few blows, and then, from outside the frame, Sonder appears, wordlessly munching on his Pringles. Without looking up, he steps between the warring passengers and just stands there, with his feet firmly planted, forming a human barrier. Still gripping his snacks in one hand, he continues eating with the other. The fighting ceases immediately—he is now in their way—and another bystander jumps in, seizing the moment to talk the parties down. The video was posted to YouTube, where it quickly went viral, garnering almost a million views (and some hilarious commentary). Why the attention? Because "Snackman" epitomized the calm, cool, courageous, and collected *up*stander we all aspire to be.

Why We Choose to Play the Bystander

In our minds, stories about power and its many abuses involve two principal characters: a victim and a perpetrator. But if we take a wider perspective, we see others on the scene, actors in minor roles or extras on the set, who are aware of what is happening but aren't sure what to do about it. I'm not talking about authority figures with the formal responsibility to prevent and punish violations (that is a topic for the final chapter). I'm talking about the rest of us who, more often than not, in the absence of a formal role that requires or permits intervention, choose to stand by and watch.

We've all been there, looking on in horror as friends, classmates, colleagues, and strangers are mistreated in ways that violate our own standards of civility and professional conduct, but feeling curiously incapable of taking action. Personally, I've been there more times than I care to admit. I've sat in meetings where intimidating speakers espoused falsehoods with great confidence, and, doubting my own sanity, I said nothing. I've pretended not to overhear offensive or grossly insensitive comments whispered by people near me. I've allowed meeting participants to bark at others inappropriately and said nothing in the moment. I've passed boxes of Kleenex to women as they described feeling bullied by people I knew; I've listened empathetically and offered advice, but chosen not to act: not to challenge, confront, or even open a dialogue with alleged perpetrators. Sometimes I stayed out of it because I believed I didn't have the clout; I was sure I too was vulnerable. Other times I wasn't sure intervention was necessary, or I wasn't sure how to intervene. And once in a while, I've stayed out of it despite the fact that I was not materially vulnerable at all, and even in some instances when I had more power than the person accused did and could almost certainly have made a difference.

It is tempting to view abusive behavior as someone else's problem: to cast ourselves in the role of the observer, or the critic in the audience. But in reality we are all players in the dramas of abuse that pollute the world we live in. Abuses of power happen in contexts where they are condoned, and every single one of us can make better choices about the roles we play in the stories that unfold in our presence.

Looking back, I count these instances among my greatest regrets and most guilt-provoking abdications of responsibility. And they felt that way even at the time. No one is proud to play the bystander. No one aspires to it, or auditions for it, and yet we seem to cast ourselves in that role all the time. Why don't we intervene when someone else is being harmed in our presence?

In the predawn hours of March 13, 1964, Kitty Genovese was stabbed, sexually assaulted, and murdered while on her way home from the bar where she had just gotten off work. According to *The New York Times* report of the incident, thirty-eight people had witnessed the attack and not one of them had intervened or even called the police. Decades later it was revealed that many details of the story were either exaggerated or false (some people had tried to help, and many of the thirty-eight didn't actually see or hear what was happening). But even so, a large body of subsequent research has since confirmed that the *bystander effect*, as it has become known, is very real.

We like to think that if we witnessed someone in that kind of danger, certainly we would try to prevent or stop it. But this is not what research shows to be true. Each of us is motivated to stay out of someone else's drama in the short run, for many good reasons: to avoid the embarrassment of overreacting, of failing to stop the abuse, or of offending someone, being injured ourselves, retaliated against, or taken advantage of. We understand that in the greater scheme of things, it is better for everyone if we can all count on one another for protection. But in the short run, self-interest tends to win out.

Social scientists know something about this—bystander behavior is at the root of many of the world's most pressing challenges. When everyone acts as though collective-action problems are someone else's responsibility, the problems get worse, and everyone suffers. These scenarios, in which we are forced to choose among actions that seem rational in the short run but are actually not rational in the long run, are a classic example of what scientists call a *social dilemma:* a scenario in which people profit if they behave selfishly while others are generous (by, in this case, taking personal risk to enforce norms). The catch, of course, in such scenarios is that if everyone is selfish, no one is protected, and bad actors continue without consequence. The only real solution to social dilemmas of all kinds is for co-actors, in this case, the bystanders on the set, to take the first risk, establish a basis of trust that facilitates others' cooperation. When individuals believe they can count on others to also make sacrifices for the good of the group, to back them up or reciprocate the gesture, they are much more likely to do so themselves.

The "Free Rider" Problem

In the workplace, it is relatively unusual to witness physical abuse, but it is not uncommon to observe acts that clearly cross a line: physical intimidation, verbal berating, personal insults, demeaning jokes, and other forms of behavior that are unnecessarily aggressive, hostile, and emotionally harmful. And it's easy to take a "free ride" in such situations, to play the bystander, to just stay out of it and let someone else take responsibility for policing group norms. But when we choose to stand idly by, it normalizes inaction and encourages everyone else to do the same.

Research on abusive behavior indicates that it rarely comes out of nowhere. And, by the same token, it rarely stops on its own. In fact, abuse typically escalates. It starts small, it breaks down its victims' defenses, and only then, when the perpetrator feels certain that he will not face resistance, does abuse become explicit and full blown. When abusers don't get away with small violations, they either change tactics or move on to other victims. Abuses of power are also contagious, like all social acts that are modeled by powerful people. When permitted to spread, the result is a toxic work context in which hostility and exploitation are accepted as an inevitable and even necessary part of how work gets done.

Bystander intervention, too, tends to start small, with one actor. And it can escalate in its way. When individuals without formal power learn how to insert themselves and make it more costly for bad actors to continue, the culture shifts: abuses of power are tolerated less, bystanders intervene more, and, as some studies show, crimes like sexual harassment and assault are less likely to occur.

To ignite this cycle, we each need to see ourselves as actors in other people's dramas. We have to acknowledge that "free riding" is an action; there is no such thing as "staying out of it," "being neutral," or "not getting involved." Free riding is a strategy designed to minimize personal risk, but it doesn't even do that in the long term. When people are allowed to abuse their power, no one is safe. A safer and more constructive approach in the long run is to notice, name it, and quietly disapprove, not just of the big, public infractions but also of the little things that can seem like no big deal but also pave the way, little by little, for much worse behavior.

The Case of the Red Stiletto

I have a colleague—now a good friend—who used to keep his office door propped open with a gadget that some creative (and probably male) designer had convincingly fashioned in the form of a woman's red stiletto shoe. It was clever in its way and surely a great conversation piece. But every time I walked past, it made me feel a little uneasy: the sight of a single woman's red, high-heeled shoe, apparently kicked off on the way into his office. It was not the shoe, per se, of course. It was what the presence of the shoe in that context implied and the ideas it sparked in my mind: that someone (maybe someone I knew!) had rushed in, torn off her clothes, and perhaps was having a romp in there (maybe on his desk!) at that very moment. I got the joke, but as one of a very small number of female faculty in the school at the time, I also knew I was not meant to be in on it. It was like a wink and a nudge from one guy to another, the kind of frat-house banter or "locker room talk" that seems harmless but assumes there are no women around who might object to being sexualized at work or harmed by it—at least, no women who matter.

I would not describe the case of the red stiletto as an abuse of power, exactly, or even necessarily at all. But I would describe it as a case in which a powerful person quietly, subtly, and probably unintentionally gave a nod to the idea of the workplace as a setting for sexual conquest. It sent the message that having sex in your office was something that could happen here; that if you went into that office, it might happen now; that it was fun to reference women as sex objects at work and that doing so would reflect well on you. And hey, who knew which of your female coworkers might be game?

The shoe was just a prop, but like all props on all stages, it was chosen as a symbol of something; it was suggestive and set a tone. Psychologists would call it a *prime*—a stimulus that upon exposure automatically triggers thoughts about related ideas—in this case, women in (and out of) red stiletto heels. Of course, people are allowed to walk the halls of the Stanford GSB thinking whatever they want. The problem is that my own research (and that of others) has found that this type of sexual priming and the thoughts it activates make men more likely to view female coworkers as sex objects, to evaluate them more on their sexual attractiveness than on their competence, to feel sexual attraction toward female subordinates, and even to engage in harassment while in a position of power.

I walked by that thing for months, maybe years, without even considering saying something to its owner, or anyone else. On one hand, it was just a gag. But on the other hand, it made me feel self-conscious—it made me think about what I was wearing, and whether it was too sexy, or not sexy enough, in a context where I had more important things to think about. And what about the other women working in the building? Professionally, he and I were more or less equals. But what about the staff, his assistant, or the many female students who went to his office seeking his advice? I could have asked him about it, teased him about it, or confessed that it made me feel weird. I could have just quietly snatched it on my way down the hall and shoved it in an office drawer and no one would have been the wiser. But instead, I chose to play the bystander.

One day, another male colleague asked me what I thought about the doorstop and I told him. The next day, it was gone.

Often, one of the trickiest challenges in dealing with a question-
able act by a powerful person is identifying it and seeing it for what
it is. Not all instances are cut-and-dried, and in some situations, it's
not always clear whether any lines have been crossed. What if the
actor did not intend to make anyone uncomfortable? What if
the target doesn't seem to be bothered or isn't identifiable? What
if the relationship appears to be consensual? What if the senator just
made an inappropriate comment because he's "from a different generation" when such things were tolerated? In the absence of clear
lines that mark where legitimate uses of power cross over into murk-
ier territory, we look to others for cues about how we should be responding. And when no one else is noticing, or acting like something
bad is happening, we count this as social proof that nothing bad is
happening. As one study showed, if you smell smoke in a crowded
room but no one else is screaming "Fire!" (literally, in the study,
though this holds true figuratively as well) you are likely to assume
there is no emergency and stay quiet to avoid being the fool who
made a big deal about nothing.

In his book *The Power of Noticing,* Harvard Business School professor and decision-making expert Max Bazerman observes how
easy it is to ignore the feeling that something is "off." He describes
an incident from his own life in which he was inappropriately pres-
sured to revise his testimony as an expert witness in a federal Justice
Department case against the tobacco industry. He refused but also
failed to report the incident. Later, he learned that another witness
had testified on the record that the Justice Department had pres-
sured him to change his testimony in the same case, and it forced
Bazerman to reflect on why he himself hadn't taken action to address what, in retrospect, was clearly an abuse of judicial power.
Often, he concluded, when we are busy or overwhelmed, we tend to
overlook or ignore the signals that something has taken a wrong

turn. This is understandable, but it also makes us complicit in allowing abuses of power to continue.

There is also the real danger of overreacting and destroying relationships, reputations, and careers by alleging abuse without just cause. What if the accused denies it, or there's ambiguity about exactly what went on (there almost always is)? What if the accused never intended to hurt anyone? (This is often true; abuses of power are designed to make the perpetrator feel good, not make the victim feel bad.) We live in a culture where people are presumed innocent until proven guilty, and especially when we care about the people we are accusing, we tend to err on the side of caution.

All of these uncertainties may be real, but at the same time they legitimize doing nothing to hold people accountable for how they behave and the effects of their behavior on other people. And when we don't act, and then espouse rationalizations like these, we are not just standing by while abuse occurs. We are enabling abuse.

Becoming an Upstander

When people talk about working on handling power better, this is not usually what they mean. As David McClelland has noted, most professional adults associate working on power with learning to stand up for themselves. But a more mature approach to power, he observed, is to view having power as a duty and an opportunity to stand up for others. The Irish American diplomat Samantha Power described this as being an *upstander*.

Being an upstander requires a mental shift. It requires learning to see yourself as a member of a community—not a lone actor, neither a victim nor a villain, but rather a guardian: someone who is willing to expend social capital and use power on someone else's behalf, not just to be kind or altruistic, or as part of a quid pro quo, but because this kind of individual risk taking is necessary for the group to prosper and thrive. Playing the upstander can feel risky, and sometimes it is. But when you take the high road by speaking up for others, you can also be rewarded for it. You earn status and respect, you become a role model, and others aspire to join you on higher ground. And it's not just that. We often think that if we only felt more powerful, we would be more likely to intervene in one another's dramas. Yet research tells us it's the other way around: when we take action to protect or take care of others, that makes us feel more powerful. Like an actor, an upstander focuses on taking action, on doing something that will have consequences in spite of one's fears, not because it is the best way to win a contest for status and power. An upstander stands up for others because taking action on behalf of one's group is what an upstander *does*. It's the only way to play the part.

When talk is cheap, and when it adds value. When abuse of power happens, there are usually "reporters" around. These are people who talk about what is happening as though they are reporting on the weather. The talk is just talk, and the speaker is detached from the situation, as though these things are acts of God or nature and therefore completely out of our hands. Reporters may imagine they are playing a useful role when they talk about what they know, about how they saw it happen, how they saw it coming (or didn't), why it happened, who is at fault, how they understand what is really going on, and how complicated it is. But in reality, when people have these conversations backstage, or offline, in contexts where there is no chance that what they say will have any constructive impact beyond elevating their own status as people "in the know," they are not engaging in useful reporting; they are engaging in gossip, which has little purpose other than to justify their inaction, claim expertise based on "insider" status, and elevate themselves above the fray. It's an opportunity to claim the moral high ground by expressing outrage over what is happening, distancing oneself from the bad guy in public, blaming the victim (who did things we would never have done to cause her own misfortune), or clearing one's conscience by expressing disapproval, without putting an ounce of skin in the game. Gossip without a higher purpose is self-serving, even when it comes out of genuine concern. Put another way, talk is cheap, when unaccompanied by action that benefits someone other than ourselves.

What differentiates reporters from upstanders, who actually make a difference in organizations, communities, and other contexts where abuse happens? Reporters are anchored on their own experience and outcomes. Upstanders—activists, allies, and guardians—are anchored on the experience and outcomes of others. Like all good actors, they have moved off themselves and are focused on the context, the community, and the cast of characters around them. An upstander speaks out in a way that is useful to others—by consoling a victim, objecting in real time to an offensive remark, telling a perpetrator offline that his comments were unwelcome, or reporting the abuse to someone who has a formal responsibility to do something about it. And an upstander does these things not because there is no risk to them personally, but despite the very real possibility that standing up exposes the actor to risk.

If we want to live in a world where people are motivated to take care—instead of taking advantage—of one another, we have to think differently about the parts we are playing in the abuse stories that happen all around us. To be an upstander instead of a bystander, you have to commit to acting and playing that role. Ideally, when one person is using power to demean another unfairly, you try to do something right then and there, in public. Try to notice what is happening, name it, or stop it, or even provide a distraction (this is a recommended approach to stopping sexual assault on campus). If you can't, do something helpful later. Tell a superior. Take the victim to lunch. Ask the perpetrator, in private, how he or she is doing. These are some of the small acts that define how norms get changed, and that define how we learn to behave ourselves in the contexts we inhabit. Cultures are defined from the top down, but the most powerful cultural changes tend to come from the bottom up. By taking little actions every day that feel risky but in reality are usually not, we can encourage other bystanders to do the same.

Take Roles Seriously

Stanford psychologist Dale Miller has observed that often the choice to intervene or not depends not just on how much we care about what is happening, but also on whether we feel we have the "psychological standing" to step in. In other words, what prevents many people from getting involved in other people's dramas is the sense that they do not have license to do so. And the more powerless we feel, the more we assume that someone more powerful than we are, or someone closer to the parties than we are, who has the formal right or standing to disapprove or intervene, should take responsibility. This is a great illustration of why roles are so important. Roles legitimize intervention on behalf of someone else. And the more narrowly we define our roles, the more we are likely to figure *It's not my job*.

A number of formal interventions that have been designed to curb abuses of power—including sexual assault, harassment, and discrimination at work—rely on enlisting persons of influence (POIs) in the effort. Specifically, high-status actors in an organization or a community are identified and asked to commit to upstander training, as a way of trying to spread the idea of intervening on others' behalf as something that admired people do. A POI is a source of peer pressure. So it can be more effective to engage POIs—who tend to have social power based on status—as allies in the effort to protect more vulnerable populations. Interventions that enlist actors who are already rich in status tend to catch on more quickly and have greater impact than those that start at the fringes (which probably require more courage and put upstanders at greater risk).

The Green Dot program, for example, employs a POI tactic by recruiting and training college students with high social status (e.g., athletes, student leaders) in sexual assault prevention efforts on campus. And now this approach is being tried in the business world as a method for reducing gender bias. Shelley Correll, a Stanford sociologist and former director of the Clayman Institute for Gender Research on campus, has been working with large technology firms to help them reduce bias against female employees in hiring, promotions, and evaluation processes. As the consulting and intervention efforts began, Correll and her colleagues experimented with different approaches to engaging men as allies and found there was wide variation in enthusiasm for the effort among the men. Some were very enthusiastic and eager to solve the problem of gender bias in their organization, while others were more reluctant to get involved personally. So they did some investigating, discovered who among the enthusiastic men was already among the most widely respected, and asked them to help recruit their more reluctant peers. Correll, who is studying the effects of such interventions, is finding that "it is much easier to get reluctant men on board when the guys they admire most are already there."

Acting as an "ally" is another powerful way to play the upstander role. Research finds that when the targets of gender bias report a violation themselves, it can be harder to trust. But when a peer reports a violation on behalf of a target, there is less potential blowback. The impact of many types of activism is undermined by the perception that, for example, women standing up for other women, or LGBTQ employees advocating for others who identify as LGBTQ, are acting out of self-interest and as an expression of an identity that others don't share. Unfortunately, the result is that often women's rights or LGBTQ rights can be marginalized as someone else's issue. But when, for example, straight white men begin standing up for more vulnerable members of the community, they receive extra status for being willing to risk their own social standing on behalf of others. And this can encourage others to take these same kinds of actions.

Research by Professor Elizabeth Morrison at NYU on organizational citizenship behaviors has carefully examined what leads some employees to engage in prosocial behaviors—like helping colleagues and taking on additional tasks and projects that are not a clear part of the job description. In part, it is a question of identity and how people define their work roles: Do they think of themselves as members of a cast whose job is to support others' performances, or as solo actors who should stay focused on how they themselves are doing? When we define ourselves as actors in a collective production, we are more likely to take risks on behalf of co-members. This process of reimagining our work roles is what my colleague Justin Berg calls *job crafting*, and he finds that people often naturally find greater meaning and purpose in their work by defining their jobs in terms of not just business-related tasks (e.g., programming, recruiting, or marketing) but also "extra-role" behaviors (e.g., being inclusive, being a mentor or a sponsor, being a team player, or being an upstander) that are more elevating and affirming of how they like to define themselves as people.

One of the most reliable ways to incite prosocial behavior in bystanders is to create a new and clearly defined role for them to play. The Guardian Angels—a self-organized group of red-beret-wearing volunteers in New York City who patrol the subways in dangerous neighborhoods—are a perfect example of how new roles can be invented for the purpose of empowering bystanders to stop abuse in their communities. Regional chapters operate under standard rules, regulations, and training, and a clear chain of command, with each volunteer assigned and reporting to a Patrol Leader. The Guardian Angels do not carry weapons, and they have no legitimate law enforcement authority, yet over the years, they have had a measurable impact on reducing crime. In some cases they tracked down repeat offenders and detained them until the police could get there. But often, their mere presence—the knowledge that there were people watching what was happening in the community and were prepared to take action to stop it—had a powerful deterrent effect. People behave badly when they think they can get away with it. The presence of citizens wearing a badge and a beret is a visible reminder and a warning that there are witnesses out there who are prepared to intervene to keep the community safe.

Even without the badge and beret, standing up for others tends to stop bad behavior. And there are many ways to do it.

Join a posse. "There's power in numbers" sounds like a cliché, but it's true and important to recognize. Take the case of Harvey Weinstein, for example. Weinstein was able to get away with abusing young actresses not just because of his stature and reputation but also because by imposing on his victims one at a time, in private, he prevented them from seeing that they had compatriots. They felt powerless, until actresses who had achieved enough power and status that Weinstein could no longer hurt them professionally began to speak out against him, one after another. And once there are multiple voices making the same accusations, a single claim is much harder to dismiss. A similar dynamic occurred in the case of Larry Nassar, the doctor who abused many, many elite gymnasts he was supposed to be caring for. As the women huddled together in the courtroom, presenting a united front, the context shifted, and so did the balance of power.

On more than a few occasions, I've been approached by students seeking advice about how to deal with a speaker who makes sexist remarks in class. "Can't we get the administration to do something?" they ask. My advice to them is always the same. Try to stop it yourselves, I tell them, by building a coalition. Agree with interested classmates ahead of time what kinds of behavior are unacceptable, and commit to a collective response: if those behaviors occur, everyone gets up and leaves together. Of course, anytime I'm informed of an incident in which the accused people are named I am required to report that to a university compliance office. But unfortunately, faculty and administrators don't always act on individual complaints about a speaker for reasons we have already discussed, and often, one voice doesn't rise to the level of an emergency. One person is easily dismissed as "too sensitive." A group of students walking out in the middle of class, however, raises the stakes. It tells an entirely different story.

Communication and collaboration are key for any coordinated action, particularly when dealing with abuses of power. Studies show that when people simply talk to one another before deciding whether to sacrifice personal gains for the good of the group, they are much more likely to do so. Communication increases trust, and it allows people to work together strategically: to make commitments to one another, to divide and conquer, to play good cop/bad cop, and so on. A great example of how this can work is a case from the 1980s in which a hardworking and high-performing female attorney at a large law firm was repeatedly (and unfairly) passed over for promotion to partner. So the secretaries made a pact: they advised their bosses, all at once, that if she was not made partner at the next opportunity, they would all stop coming to work. Sure enough, at the next opportunity the attorney was promoted to partner.

I recently heard a story about how, in the wake of the #MeToo movement, a female executive at a large company where gender inequities were rampant used the same kind of strategy. Having watched many individual women lodge complaints of various kinds with HR to no avail over the years, she decided to quietly organize a collective action. She reached out to her female contacts and urged them to submit their individual complaints en masse—at exactly the same time on the same day. She reports that it was like dropping a bomb. It sent HR scrambling, and within weeks, salary adjustments had been made, perpetrators had been fired or put on leave, and the corrections changed the culture in the firm irrevocably.

Individual bystanders may play bit parts in the drama of abuse, but as part of a posse, they become central players. Research on minority influence shows that even two dissenting voices make a much more powerful statement than a single voice dissenting alone. They are more credible, harder to dismiss, and at lower risk for retaliation. It is easy to fire or silence an individual whistle-blower, but it is not easy to function without any executive assistants on hand.

These efforts provide helpful guidance for how to address bullying, discrimination, sexual harassment, and assault in any kind of group or organization. By training bystanders to recognize, address, and report problematic interactions, we can change how we collectively respond to actions that cross the line and make hierarchical organizational contexts feel unsafe. It's not just the responsible choice; it's also the smarter choice for anyone who has a personal stake in creating environments where abuses of power are a less satisfying option than they currently seem to be.

Try humor. Abuse is no laughing matter, but a lighthearted approach can be an effective way of policing the boundaries of civility. Once, when I was a newly minted assistant professor, one of my MBA students snuck up close behind me in the cafeteria and put his hands on my waist to say hello. As I turned to see who had so boldly invaded my space, another student comically sprinted over and smacked his hands away. "Dude!" he laughed. "Don't touch her! What are you thinking?" It was a friendly, but firm, intervention.

Fran Sepler, a sexual harassment consultant who testified recently at EEOC hearings on the subject, similarly recommends using a witty jab to disrupt bad behavior in meetings. Asking "What year is this? 1970?" in response to a sexist comment is one of my personal favorites.

Recently, I heard a story from a salesperson who works in the technology industry that validated this advice. He was at a business conference and late one night, at the bar, a colleague started to rank the women at his company according to whom he would most like to sleep with. My friend (who is the father of a toddler) quickly intervened by proclaiming, in his best angry-dad voice, "That's it! Time out! I think you had better go to your room now." Everyone laughed, and the ranking exercise was over.

Teasing may feel like too light a touch, but in fact, it is very powerful. My collaborator Dacher Keltner, who studies teasing as a social dynamic, has described how it can be a way of speaking truth to power while simultaneously strengthening the relationship. The key is to find a way to do it that allows the offender to be in on the joke. You might, for example, tease a colleague about the fact that his subordinates are afraid of him—which acknowledges his power, while suggesting that its impact is not necessarily something to be proud of. Teasing is playing power up in an inclusive way: it can re-affirm someone's belonging to the group while taking them down a notch at the same time.

Build a penalty box. On the occasion of her recent retirement from Stanford, I described Professor Maggie Neale as "firm, but fair." One of the ways she displays this quality is by using what she calls "the penalty box." When someone in her orbit misbehaves, she just takes them out of the game by boxing them out of her professional circle—

temporarily. It's never a secret; you know when you are in there and others know too because she'll talk about it. She and I have been close colleagues for twenty-five years, so we have a lot of history. I'll ask, for example, *How's so-and-so?* And she'll say, *In the penalty box.* And we'll chuckle. Sometimes she'll tell me why. Putting someone in the penalty box, much like teasing, lets the perpetrator know that they are part of her circle and that their actions matter, but it also puts them on notice: behave yourself, or you are out.

The penalty box is a sanction that has teeth while leaving room for offenders to redeem themselves. It is not a permanent ostracism. It clearly names the infraction, but treats it—at least the first time—as though it is forgivable. The penalty box is also a perfect example of what is known as a tit-for-tat strategy: you play nice as long as others play nice, but if someone plays rough, you respond in kind, immediately. This is a great way to approach policing misuses of power in your circle. Give people the benefit of the doubt, but if your trust is violated, the gloves come off. And a key aspect of this strategy is that you don't hold a grudge: once the bad behavior stops and there is an obvious attempt to do better, you forgive and play nice again immediately.

It's tempting to believe that if we ignore bad behavior that is not directed at us, it will go away. But research suggests this is not the case. It's straight out of a Motivation 101 textbook—people will continue to do the thing that pays off, not just in terms of financial reward and promotions, but in terms of social status. The thing is, to affect another person's status, you have to change how you behave toward that person. You have to do something to encourage good behavior and to discourage bad behavior; without action, how you feel about what one person does to someone else is irrelevant. People who use their power well, who take risks to support others (especially in public), should be acknowledged and thanked. In order to be discouraged, those who abuse their power must experience a negative consequence; we've discussed a number of ways this can be accomplished. You don't have to be formally in charge to do any of this. Even without the authority to promote or fire, or to control access to monetary outcomes, we all have the power to enforce social norms with our own reactions to what is happening around us. In a group of peers, for example, we make decisions every day about who is or isn't included in lunch plans or excursions to happy hour or meetings that take place behind closed doors, who's in the group chat, whose texts we respond to and whose we let hang. Shutting someone out, even temporarily, is a very effective way to discourage misuses of power locally, where we all live and work, among peers. To use our own power well, we have to be willing to accept the roles we play in other people's dramas.

Act like you care. For the first time in history, sexual misconduct in the halls of power is no longer par for the course. Abuses of power that were once silently tolerated or shrugged off with excuses like "Boys will be boys" are now widely viewed as serious offenses, with real victims and real consequences. As a result, there is more pressure than ever to hold men accountable.

By the same token, there are now real payoffs for being known as the guy, or the boss, or the CEO who supports the advancement of women. We have reached a point in many sectors (not all) where men gain more status from sharing power with women than from lording it over them. The balance of power is shifting.

When I was studying at the University of Illinois a few decades ago, I cannot recall working with or taking a class from a single female professor in my entire five years there. In that eight-story building full of research psychologists, there were just a handful—stars like Carol Dweck and Louise Fitzgerald, a sexual harassment expert. Of course, all of the administrative assistants were lovely, extremely competent, and (one can only assume) overqualified women. Meanwhile, I had female classmates who recounted how they had come out of meetings crying, feeling demeaned, unfairly judged, and sometimes sexually targeted by members of the male faculty. It wasn't common, but it wasn't unheard of either.

Over the past few years I've wondered, particularly in light of recent events, how I managed to emerge from that environment more or less unscathed. The answer is that I was very fortunate. I knew it then, but I understand it now. Through a series of accidents, I found my way into a program that was extremely hospitable to me, and one in which I had men—professors, co-authors, statistical advisors, thesis readers, and so on—not just looming over me, but looking out for me. These men all had status and power and could have taken advantage of it, but instead, they took me under their wing. They graded my work and gave me feedback, showed me how to analyze my data, how to argue with an editor, how to write a journal article, and how to review one. They wrote helpful letters of recommendation—a tremendous source of power for any supervisor—and asked for nothing (except my hard work) in exchange. They made working with female subordinates look easy. There were other guys around too, postdocs, visiting scholars, and more advanced graduate students who had status without formal power, who knew the ropes and were hip to what was happening, and treated the female students with respect and admiration, like equals, fellow human beings. To me, they were like big brothers. They asked how we were doing, told us whom to watch out for, and when they felt someone crossed the line in their dealings with us, they would let us know. On occasion, when we all went out for beer in mixed company, they told stories, ribbed one another, and in doing so reminded everyone where the lines were. They were willing to risk ruffling feathers, even those of the more senior faculty members who still held all the cards.

While writing this book, I reached out to some of those guys who looked out for my safety and well-being back then. I wanted to know why they did it. More generally, I wanted to know what motivates a bystander to want to use the power he has responsibly, to protect those with less power, even when it is personally risky for him.

What they described was a feeling of solidarity, of community; as one of them put it, "I identified as part of a group of graduate students who were in the trenches together."

The lesson in this story is that abuses of power can be effectively policed, and perhaps even controlled, when we can choose to see ourselves as actors rather than spectators, and members of a cast rather than the audience. It is not a question of who cares and who doesn't, or whether you care or not. Most people do care about abuses of power that happen around them. It is a question of learning to *act* like you care.

10

How to Use Power
While Playing the Lead

During the height of the #MeToo movement, Speaker of the House Paul Ryan was asked by an NPR reporter what should be done to address the problem of pervasive sexual misconduct on Capitol Hill. "We are elected officials," said Ryan; "we should be held to a higher standard." The reporter cut in: "What is the standard?" "Well, that's a good question," Ryan said. "I think here in Congress, we should hold ourselves to standards that we expect of other people and we should set high standards for ourselves so that we can be role models and set examples, and clearly people have been falling short of that and I think we always have to endeavor to do a better job on that."

Huh?

It's not his fault that he didn't really have an answer. I've never heard anyone successfully articulate the standard to which powerholders should be held. In fact, I'm still working on it myself. We don't have the vocabulary for it or even know exactly what it looks like. That's because we don't pay nearly as much attention to people who use power well as to those who don't. When people use power well, it doesn't make news. As a result, we don't have as clear a picture of what it means to be an effective power-holder, or what we ourselves could do differently to be one of them.

Like Ryan, most people can articulate what *not* to do in positions of power—don't show off, don't take advantage of people, don't use your position for personal gain—but this "what not to do" approach to changing behavior, psychologists know, is not helpful and may even make things worse. Studies by the late Dan Wegner at Harvard showed reliably that when people tell themselves *not* to do something, they are inadvertently more likely to do it, because thinking about not doing something automatically activates the idea of doing that very thing. The classic demonstration: If I tell you "Don't think of a white bear," what happens next? You think of a white bear. It's a neat demonstration with real implications, Wegner's research found, for trying to curb sexual misconduct in the halls of power. In one experiment, participants were instructed to play cards and at the same time play footsie under the table. He told some participants to try to hide what they were doing, while others were free to "footsie" away without restraint. Who do you think felt more attracted to their partners afterward? The ones who tried not to show they were "flirting."

So, when playing the lead, it is not enough to know what *not* to do. Instead, we need to channel the energy that accompanies power into socially constructive action. And in the absence of a clear standard or set of expectations for how to do so, we should not be surprised that people fall short. It is hard to be what you can't see.

Inspiration for Playing the Lead

We all need role models. And when looking for inspiration, the worst place to look, unfortunately, is in the news. Famous people are often infamous. Similarly, it is not enough to remind ourselves of the people in our lives we do *not* want to emulate, although these kinds of people tend to come to mind first when we think about power. Instead, when seeking inspiration, it is much better to ask yourself: *Who are the people in my life who have used their power in a way that made a real difference for me?*

I met the late, great Joe McGrath at a time when I knew of him as the famous—not infamous—social psychologist my dad (also a professor and social psychologist) admired, but Joe did not know me. I was approaching thirty, without any significant attachments, and was contemplating some scary commitments: going back to school for five years, a career in research and teaching that might or might not suit me, and a move from the East Coast to the cornfields. I had flown out to Chicago, rented a car, and set off to visit some of the big Midwestern psychology departments. I didn't tell anyone I was coming.

My first stop was the University of Illinois at Urbana-Champaign. I found my way to the psychology building and wandered in, like a tourist, looking for the names my dad had given me and trying to get a feel for the place. At one point, I paused in the middle of the second-floor hallway to look down at the building's internal courtyard. When I looked up there was a man approaching, silent in his black sneakers, half smiling. "Can I help you find something?" he asked.

He was a soft-spoken, geeky professor who, with his thick glasses, pocket protector, and sensible slacks cinched tight at the waist, looked straight out of central casting. I told him that I was between careers, working as a waitress, and considering applying to graduate school. He unlocked the door to his tiny, cluttered office, which smelled of burnt coffee, and invited me in. He found me an hour of his time and attention, and in the space Joe created, I found what I was looking for.

I applied to the University of Illinois, was admitted, and was assigned to work as a research assistant on one of Joe's grants. I arrived feeling unprepared. But Joe saw something in me and was determined to find out what it was. On one hand, he had very high standards; Joe never let anything go. On the other, I discovered I couldn't ever really let him down. He judged my work harshly but never my person. His support was not contingent on my success or failure. He was always in my corner, encouraging, advising, in ways that felt a lot like coaching: he would scratch *Go! Go! Go!* in red ink in the margins of a paper he liked, or *Ack!* if I took a wrong turn. He would dust me off if I took a blow and send me right back out there.

We spent a lot of time together. We had weekly one-on-one meetings alone in his office, and sometimes we met at his home, where we'd sink into deep chairs in the small office adjacent to his kitchen and talk about work. One summer, Joe and his wife, Marion, invited me and a couple of other students to their lake cottage in the Michigan outback. We stayed in the guest house; Joe and Marion stayed in the main cabin. We took long walks in the woods and talked about ideas while swatting at clouds of mosquitoes. My relationship with Joe was very close, it was very warm, and it was entirely safe, without any hint of impropriety. I had never felt more competent, more secure, or more capable. Under his tutelage, I began to thrive.

A lot of us students—women especially—adored him, but not everyone did. Joe was a fighter; if you didn't play by his rules, the gloves came off. He was extremely open-minded in most ways, except when it came to his principles. He knew how to tread lightly, but he did not hesitate to play the heavy if he thought he needed to. Joe was kind, but you couldn't exploit him (or anyone he felt responsible for).

I have no idea how Joe felt about his own power, but I know for sure that he was aware of it, because he was mindful about how he used it. Joe created safe spaces in which his students could learn without fear of taking risks. He treated people with equal respect while acknowledging their unequal power. He valued intelligence, hard work, and excellence, but he did not have an elitist bone in his body. He took his work seriously, but never himself. Joe McGrath defined the standard, for me, to which all power-holders should be held.

The Standard of Beneficence

Beneficence is a principle in applied ethics that obligates individuals in high-power roles to prioritize the welfare of less powerful others. In research contexts, for example, the term refers to the standard for how researchers should treat their subjects. In business, beneficence implies using power to benefit constituents, to achieve financial results in a way that respects the rights of employees and customers. Beneficence is treating power not just as a resource to accumulate or wield with impunity but as a resource to invest in other people. The standard of beneficence takes the possession of power for granted. It assumes the actor has enough power already and that the measure of a person is not how much power one has but what one uses power for.

Playing the lead. Shakespeare wrote that all the world's a stage, and at the risk of cheapening his sentiment, I want to suggest that organizations are, in large part, theater. To use power well as an actor in a high-power role, you have to play the lead. It has been said that there are two things "the leader" should never delegate: one is the vision, and the other is the role. What does this mean? The highest-ranking group member in any context must use the status, visibility, and power that come with the position to provide meaning by making sense of a chaotic world for everyone else. The leader must appear onstage, often, to articulate a direction and a destination that keeps individual actors focused on the shared objectives that bind them together. Without a clear, elevating, and shared purpose, organizations collapse into their lowest common denominator. They become a battleground for those who feel the least secure, who need validation, and who will grab first at the chance to do something that elevates their importance.

The way a leader uses power sets the stage for everyone else. And in organizations where the most powerful members are reluctant to take a stand in articulating a vision, everyone else competes for control, tries to build an empire, and works at cross-purposes. Without a clear sense of direction coming down from the top, the organization spins its wheels and nothing productive or meaningful ever gets done. And without a clear shared purpose, individuals are left to pursue their own purposes so that the work they are doing has meaning.

Sometimes, power-holders try to avoid these responsibilities for fear of seeming too autocratic, domineering, or self-aggrandizing (or of just being wrong). It is not uncommon, for example, for a new leader to delegate the process of defining the vision, goals, or strategy, as a way of trying to learn and maximize buy-in. This is almost always a mistake. There is certainly nothing wrong with finding out what others in the organization think is important and using their input to inform strategic choices. But the person in charge has a responsibility to lead, which means taking the risk of stepping out in front.

To play the leading role in any context, you also have to be a role model, whether you see yourself that way or not. You have to show the others how it's done, to set an example of how to behave like a person who is worthy of respect and admiration. As organizational scholars Lee Bolman and Terrence Deal write in their book *Refram-*

ing Organizations, when you view leadership as a role or a part in which you have been cast, you realize that the most carefully watched actors in an organization are living, breathing symbols of the organization's most sacred values. A powerful leader does not just drive results. The role of the leader is to "reassure, foster belief in the organization's purposes, and cultivate hope and faith." In other words, a leader will stand for something, intentionally or not.

How to Stand for Something

Lieutenant General Jay Silveria of the U.S. Air Force definitely gets it. For a great example of how to use a powerful role to create a culture of beneficence, check him out on YouTube. But first, a bit of background.

In the fall of 2017, as a new school year was commencing at the highly competitive U.S. Air Force Academy preparatory academy in Colorado Springs, five black cadet candidates found racist slurs scrawled on their message boards. Silveria sprang into action by showing up in uniform at an assembly of 4,000 cadets and 1,500 faculty and staff. "If you are outraged," he told the audience, "then you are in the right place." He defined the insult to those five cadets as a personal insult to each and every one of them. "Some of you may think that that happened down in the prep school and doesn't apply to us," he said. An assault on the racial diversity those cadets brought to their class was an assault on the military, he said, because diversity is what gives the military its power. "This is our institution, and no one can take away our values." Lots of leaders say these things, but they don't do what he did toward the end of his speech. "Reach for your phones," he said, urging them to record what he was saying in case they needed to use his words at another time. He then summed it up: "If you can't treat someone with dignity and respect, then get out."

To use power well, in the role of the leader, is to provide what hostage negotiator George Kohlrieser calls a "secure base"; that is, "a person, place, goal or object that provides a sense of protection, safety and caring, and offers a source of inspiration and energy for daring, exploration, risk taking and seeking challenge." Drawing on British researcher John Bowlby's attachment theory, Kohlrieser writes that individuals who feel securely attached to authority figures are more psychologically secure themselves. They act with a wisdom and maturity that is less evident in those who feel more needy. And why is this an important outcome in organizations? Because the person in power is not just accountable for his own behavior. The person in power is accountable for the abuse that happens on his watch.

This is why it's so important to get the right people in the big roles. To create a culture where people feel safe and capable of optimal performance, it's not enough for the leader to set the direction and play the lead. It is important to make sure that other organization members are rewarded, promoted, and cast in big roles based on the standards of beneficence and maturity.

The Perils of Typecasting

Who gets the big roles in organizations, and how? Who gets noticed? Who gets recommended? Which interpersonal qualities are most valued and rewarded? When making casting decisions, we love the idea of using merit as an objective criterion. But what defines a good performance is highly subjective.

In life, as in the theater, certain kinds of people tend to get stuck playing certain kinds of roles. This happens because we draw on what we have seen before and choose people who "look the part." In the theater this is called typecasting. Everywhere else, it's called bias.

The prevalence of typecasting in all kinds of roles is well documented. For example, research on implicit bias shows that people who belong to "higher-status" social groups are expected to play leading roles, while those in "lower-status" social groups are expected to play supporting ones. Why? Because this is how it has always been. Psychologists have long observed that most people believe in a just world; that is, we tend to assume without thinking that hierarchies reflect a fair and unbiased ordering on the basis of merit. This belief in a "just world" is a misconception that provides a sense of psychic security by implying that things are as they should be, even when deeper consideration suggests otherwise.

The implications of this are widely known: everywhere we look, we see companies mirroring the status ordering in society, with white men outnumbering other kinds of people in the biggest organizational roles in a way that is not representative of the talent pool. Why? Companies and organizations tend to cast people who look and act like the majority of high-ranking people who are already there. So if an organization is run by white men, that organization is likely to hire more white men into "leadership track" positions and promote them more readily.

In the entertainment industry, typecasting, or choosing an actor based on whether they are the right "type" to play a certain role, makes a certain kind of sense. Presumably, audiences prefer and will pay more to see certain types of actors as "leading men" and "leading ladies." Beyond the worlds of stage and screen, however, casting based on "type" is harder to explain and even harder to justify. Still, it seems to work the same way. It is exceedingly common in organizations (and politics) for decision makers (and voters) to use the qualities that define who looks most like a leader—based on physical, nonverbal indicators of confidence, dominance, extraversion, physical strength, and masculinity—as markers of leadership potential. These qualities are all part of what it means to have "executive presence," which is a social construct defined in large part by gender-role stereotypes, but also one that can be learned after someone is cast in a high-power role, yet is considered a legitimate criterion for hiring and promotions. These qualities absolutely predict the outcomes of casting decisions in organizations. Yet they have no relationship whatsoever to how an actor will actually perform in the role.

With men still holding more power politically, economically, and professionally than women, perhaps it's no surprise that we associate power with masculinity and that we prefer to see strong, dominant-looking male actors in high-power roles. Masculine behavior is defined by dominance, conceptually. Studies show that men as a group are thought of as more decisive, active, and assertive than women, whereas women are thought of as more caring and nurturing than men.

In addition, though, we think that since men *are* more dominant and women *are* more nurturing, this is how things *should be*. So men are also expected to act tough, display more confidence, and assert themselves based on gender norms, and when a man acts dominant it looks like he is acting how he is supposed to act. The result is that men play power up more than women, on average: they tend to speak more in mixed groups, to make more noise, to express themselves with greater confidence and take up more physical space. For women, gender norms dictate the opposite. Women who act kind and friendly are doing what they are "supposed" to do. And for this reason, we don't ascribe leadership qualities (when defined in terms of dominance) to women as regularly even if the potential is there, and when we do, we don't trust women who act assertive, confident, and decisive, like leaders. Women learn that deference and submissiveness are safer strategies, in terms of status and establishing trust. So when dominance is used as a standard for leadership potential, many women don't seem to fit the bill.

When we define leadership potential in terms of dominance and masculinity, we judge leadership potential on the basis of these qualities. The problem is that while these qualities do predict ascendance into high-power roles, they fail to predict effectiveness. If we were to cast more intentionally for beneficence—which does predict effective use of power—gender might work *for* women in the casting process, instead of against them, and different kinds of men would also rise to the top.

Imagine how the world might change if the people in charge knew better and more explicitly how to select, train, evaluate, and reward job candidates using the standard of beneficence. If people were given more power and bigger roles based not just on results but also on demonstrated track records of maturity: comfort with power and power differences, the ability to compete and act aggressively when it advances others' outcomes but not all the time, to take the heat and share the spotlight, to put the group first by fighting for it, to sacrifice personal outcomes for the welfare of future generations, to act responsibly in times of crisis, to demonstrate calm under pressure, to inspire by example, to exhibit both the fortitude and the caring to make others more secure. Aren't these the kind of people we want wielding power at work, in our families, in politics, and in the rest of the world?

Casting for Beneficence

The film *Mad Max: Beyond Thunderdome* is the third film in a four-part series about a postapocalyptic future. Based loosely on William Golding's 1954 classic novel *The Lord of the Flies*, the story is about what would happen if the world ended and only children were left to build a new world. The residents of Bartertown are naïve, petty, immature, and fearful and possess childish beliefs about how the world actually works. The result is a win-or-die culture where there is no social order, no one is safe, and the children are all out for themselves. The character Dr. Dealgood puts it this way: "Thunderdome's simple. Get to the weapons. Use them any way you can. I know you won't break the rules. There aren't any."

Many organizations are like this. And in business the benefits of a win-or-die culture are widely touted. Supposedly, a culture of dog-eat-dog competition motivates individuals to do their best. But recent studies find that it is these kinds of organizations, specifically, where the most toxic and illegal forms of abuse and harassment are most rampant. In a workplace where there are no rules, attending a meeting feels like stepping into an arena, and every interaction is a fight to the death. In a win-or-die culture, we assume others are out to get us, we are always on the defensive, we grab power at every opportunity, and we use it to take others down.

To date, no one that I know of has suggested an alternative to a win-or-die culture. So I'm going to do that now: the antidote to a win-or-die mentality is a culture of beneficence. In a culture of beneficence, the people in charge use their power to make rules, hold everyone accountable, and show every day in their actions what it means to use power for the benefit of the group. When casting for a win-or-die culture, we seek the strongest competitors. When casting for a culture of beneficence, we need to look deeper. We need to understand better where a person's competitive energy comes from and what that tells us about how she will use power when she wins. We need a new set of criteria for identifying leadership potential.

Achievement orientation. Sarah grew up in a small town in Northern Ireland during the bloody thirty-year conflict between Protestants and Catholics over who would rule the country. Her mother was the district nurse, and her father the personnel manager at the local mill. Their lives revolved around helping others, and Sarah says she learned her "people first" mentality from them.

A quintessential good girl with soft features and large brown eyes, Sarah was an outstanding student who excelled at engineering as an undergraduate and graduated in the top 10 percent of her business school class. Her first big job was at a top consulting firm where everyone wanted to work. Later she moved to a top investment bank, which was even more competitive.

Early in her career, Sarah had been advised to choose a path on which her performance would be evaluated quantitatively; that is, by the numbers. This would protect her, it was hoped, from the gender bias that might hold her back in careers that relied on more subjective performance criteria. At the bank she did very well, and her star was on the rise. But when she sought advice about how to make partner, she hit a wall. "If you want to be partner," one mentor told her, "you have to start fighting for it. Tell everyone you want the role, and be unrelenting. You have to show how hungry you are, how determined you are, and how aggressive you can be. Don't take 'Wait' for an answer."

Sarah went back to work, put her head down, and tried to check all of the boxes. She went after results, but also went about lobbying, advocating for herself, so much so that she feared she was being too pushy. After a few months, she went back to her mentor, who told her she still wasn't pushy enough.

Sarah left banking. She moved to tech, and became CFO at a billion-dollar firm that she helped to take public. Today, she is CEO of a large, profitable social media platform. Clearly, Sarah was more than capable of handling a bigger role at the investment bank. But she was not equipped to fight for partner in the way that was valued there. Instead of channeling her energy toward claiming a bigger role, she stayed focused on achieving results that would benefit others in the role she had. When this was not enough, she moved to a place where her natural strengths were more of an advantage, and things worked out very well for everyone.

It is very common to promote individuals into positions of power based on how hungry they seem. But contrary to conventional wisdom, studies find that ambition and self-promotion do not predict effective leadership. If anything, evidence suggests that the opposite may be true. The ability to play power up by lobbying, self-promoting, empire-building, and aggressively calling attention to oneself, one's achievements, and one's potential in an attempt to gain status is an important predictor of who rises in groups, and for many people it is at the heart of what is challenging about professional life. But the standard of beneficence suggests that this emphasis, in many contexts, may be misplaced. David McClelland's research showed, as one example, that professionals with a high need for power rose quickly, but their careers were prone to scandals. Those who were high in both need for power and need for achievement, however, had a different, more effective career trajectory. The need for achievement, for mastery and personal excellence, is a socializing influence on the need for power. This suggests that to create organizations in which power is used effectively, it may be useful to cast people who have shown not just that they are capable of rising quickly but also that they are interested in the quality of their performances and are willing to do their time in a lower-level position in order to learn, to hone their expertise, and to contribute (repeatedly) to something they care about.

The key to using power well is to focus on what your group needs. For some people, this comes naturally, and for others, it doesn't. Journalist Sam Walker describes how Dwight Eisenhower—who was certainly among the most popular of U.S. presidents, if not one of the most effective—never even wanted to run for president. He did it out of obligation, because his party wanted him to run. Leaders who see power as a duty rather than an opportunity to accumulate valued resources will be less focused on their own needs for status, validation, and recognition, and more on achieving outcomes that benefit everyone. Instead of using ambition as a criterion for casting people in positions of power, perhaps we should use commitment to solving other people's problems.

Commitment orientation. There is also great danger in choosing power-holders based on charisma or likability, although this is unfortunately common practice. As we have seen, managers who care more about being liked than about having impact on the groups they oversee tend to perform worse in positions of power than people who don't care so much about it.

Charisma is a magnetic force that emanates more from some people than others, and is a powerful source of interpersonal attraction. But research shows that charisma actually contributes very little to the success and survival of groups and organizations. Charisma, like dominance, also predicts who gets the big roles in organizations. But this is not rational either.

Harvard professor Rakesh Khurana, an expert on the study of charismatic leaders, writes in the *Harvard Business Review* that "because no chief executive stays in the post forever, any system of authority based on the power of an individual will ultimately be unstable. Organizations that depend on a succession of charismatic leaders are essentially relying on luck. . . .

"Charismatic leaders reject limits to their scope and authority. They rebel against all checks on their power and dismiss the rules and norms that apply to others. As a result, they can exploit the irrational desires of their followers. That's because following a charismatic leader involves more than merely acknowledging his skills—it requires full surrender." Charisma attracts attention and positive

regard. But when we cast people in positions of power based on charisma and likability, we run the risk of elevating individuals who
care more about whether others love them than the outcomes that
affect other people.

When casting for beneficence, we can focus instead on warmth.
Warmth, charisma, and likability are often used interchangeably,
but they are not at all the same. Being warm, in a position of power,
is not just about being charming, lovable, or universally adored.
Warmth is an indicator of something deeper. Warmth is about
genuine caring, commitment, reliability, and being present and
engaged, even if you are rushed, overwhelmed, introverted, or distracted. It is about demonstrating reliably that you want others to
succeed, and that you're willing to exert personal energy, take personal risk, and make personal sacrifice to make that happen.

Warmth is having the capacity to act forcefully, when needed, to
help someone else and also to act in a nonthreatening way—to both
play power up and play it down—to provide reassurance that you are
in someone else's corner, and to back it up by helping others improve, not just relying on flattery, charm, or cheap talk.

Warmth is often thought to be incompatible with competence.
But warmth as I'm defining it here, like tough love, does not undermine perceptions of competence. To the contrary, they mutually reinforce each other. Instead of relying on charm and likability when
casting individuals in powerful roles, we should consider looking
for evidence of competence plus caring and commitment to others.

Developmental maturity. Beneficence—the capacity in a high-
power actor to prioritize the welfare of less powerful others—is a
sign of developmental maturity. Yet when casting for high-power
roles, no one talks about this quality. Across cultures and psychological theories, maturity is defined as the ability to control selfish
impulses and act in ways that benefit others. A mature approach to

power, according to David McClelland, is defined the same way. Most professionals, he found, focus on gaining power for personal advancement, yet according to McClelland, this approach to power is not particularly advanced, psychologically. A more mature approach to power, he theorized, and one that is associated with successful careers based on lasting contributions to society, is marked by an awareness that power is a resource that exists outside of oneself for the purpose of solving other people's problems. When casting for leadership roles, if I'm reading McClelland correctly, this is what we should be looking for.

Developmental maturity in the realm of power looks like what sports journalist Sam Walker, author of *The Captain Class*, describes as a kind of selflessness that characterizes legendary team captains who are willing to carry the water, to fight through physical injury to achieve team success, and who possess a "kill switch" that allows them to control their emotions and channel them purposefully for the benefit of the team.

My colleague Nir Halevy calls it "in-group love," a quality that some decision makers have but others don't, which drives them to expend personal resources to advance group causes without any promise of individual payoff. Halevy uses experimental game paradigms, like the prisoner's dilemma, to study how people make choices between individual and group payoffs, and how those choices affect their status and power. Players who show they care enough about group outcomes to risk a personal loss are elevated into leadership positions, he finds, while those who try to game the system by relying on others' sacrifices are voted off the island. Peers can smell it a mile away—why can't the people who cast actors into positions of power that matter?

This way of behaving might sound irrational, but in truth it is not. A mature approach to using power across the life span is marked developmentally by a focus on protecting future generations, which, in terms of evolution, is the only approach that makes sense. And groups value this way of approaching power, as they should. In Halevy's paradigm, the students who gave up their own resources to invest in group success with no promise of any return or personal benefit were exhibiting maturity ahead of their time. There was no self-preservation in it. And although it might have seemed irrational, they were rewarded for it with status, or perceptions of leadership potential. These were the people whom groups wanted as leaders, not the ones who were selfish; that is, who were dominant or competitive in ways that benefited no one else. And not the ones who were always generous or altruistic, no matter who the beneficiary was. When a person exhibits a habit, or at least a mindset, of being loyal and committed to one group more than others, of being ready to sacrifice personal advantage or opportunity—to wield power aggressively or cede it to others—depending on what the in-group needs to succeed and thrive, that is evidence of a mature approach to power.

Beneficent Power in Everyday Life

We tend to think of power dynamics in terms of our work lives, but the truth is that they define life outside the workplace as well. Over the past few years there has been a rise in authoritarian governments around the world that has puzzled observers but makes sense to me. As societies become less stable, as the threats of resource scarcity loom ever larger, we crave order and social control. More and more people feel more and more powerless. More and more abuse and violence ensue.

Solving the problem of global inequality may not be a practical ideal, but the goal of simply managing power differences better is well within reach. People act with generosity when they feel most secure. When it comes to power, the adage *Think global and act local* is not a bad standard: to make an impact on the world, you first have to work to build trust and commitment at home.

People take care of one another when they see themselves connected, as part of a tribe. There are parts of the world in which this happens naturally, but unfortunately it's not what tends to happen here. In our culture, wealth and prosperity work against communal values. They create a sense—which I believe is false—that because we do not need one another for material survival, we are happier and more prosperous as free agents than we are as members of a collective. Research does not bear this out. In fact, countless studies show that the single greatest predictor of mental health is social connection. Thinking of ourselves as part of a community—a cast, an ensemble, a production—connects us, psychologically, to other people and to causes greater than ourselves.

We tend to think of culture as something fixed and stable. But in large part, culture is just a set of assumptions and norms about the world and how it works. Nor is culture preordained; we create cultures around us that reinforce our own goals and beliefs. Leaders and entrepreneurs do this every day, and so do teachers and parents. Whether we are building a business, educating children, or raising a family, we can all create cultures where power is used to benefit others. The key is to inspire by example, set up structures that allow people to contribute effectively, reward the good behavior, and punish the bad. In a world where it seems that we need one another less and less materially, we actually need one another more and more psychologically. Taking roles seriously is a recipe for making relationships work.

The Stories We Tell about Power—
and Why They Matter

Here's something else I've learned from hanging out with actors who tell stories about power for a living. We need to change the narrative about what it means to be a powerful person and to lead a powerful life. In great works of drama and literature, there are no stories about perfect people who start off with advantages and gracefully master the universe. No one cares about these characters; no one can relate. What makes for a compelling narrative, in the theater and in life, is the struggle: the triumph, the tragedy, and how the character has coped and endured.

The MBA students who take my class Acting with Power often wonder at first why they are being asked to play the unappealing characters who populate great plays—like the corrupt salesmen in David Mamet's *Glengarry Glen Ross,* the desperate, manipulative actresses in John Patrick Shanley's *Four Dogs and a Bone,* or the drunk, vulgar, and feuding sisters in *Top Girls* by Caryl Churchill—instead of admirable, invincible heroes, benevolent kings, and revered leaders from the annals of history. The answer is simple: no one writes plays about perfect people. Those stories would be untrue, and that would make them artistically uninteresting. A great play reveals deep, universal truths about humanity that allow us to see ourselves in one another. And in any great story, the most powerful characters are—like all of us—flawed, messy people whose weaknesses are on full display. This is why we actually care about them.

To use power well, we need to own all of what makes us human: our weaknesses as well as our strengths. And this is why the exercise of playing flawed characters on a stage is useful. When you internalize the ugly truth of a character, do things in front of an audience while "in role" that you would never condone while just "being yourself," and find it does not fundamentally change who you are, the experience can be transformative. Playing a flawed character on-stage, truthfully, is an exercise in empathy. It challenges us to understand how the good and bad come together in others, and to choose acceptance over judgment, and love over hate and fear, in our treatment of others, and of ourselves.

Does that sound Pollyannaish? Maybe it is. We can argue all day about whether people are fundamentally good or evil, and whether power accrues to the winners or the givers. But no one actually knows the answers to these questions, and, with apologies to the philosophers out there, no one can. Speaking as a psychologist, though, I do know that the only way to create the world we want to live in is to act as though we already live there. When we assume that others are out to get us, that no one can be trusted, and that we are alone in the world, we use power defensively, to protect ourselves. When we act out of fear, we create the world we are afraid of. But when we act out of hope, assuming, as I do, that others are fundamentally good and caring, we use power generously, put others first, and create a foundation of trust that makes it rational for others to do the same. To me, this is what power is for.

Acknowledgments

I am beyond grateful to my co-instructors at Stanford, with whom I have developed and delivered the course Acting with Power for over a decade. My work with these extraordinary artists—actors, improvisors, writers, and directors—has profoundly enriched my life. I have learned so much, not just about acting but about power, from these inspiring performers, brilliant coaches, and incredibly generous human beings. From Kay Kostopoulos, our guru, who was my first acting teacher and course co-founder, to Rich Cox Braden, Melissa Jones Briggs, and Dan Klein, all extraordinary teachers and masters of experiential pedagogy, who have worked tirelessly with me to improve on the basic form, to William Hall, founder of BATS Improv, and scene coach extraordinaire, to Carrie Paff, Lisa Rowland, Kevin Ralston, Janet Watson, Bobby Weinapple, and the other fantastic theater professionals who have dropped in on occasion for "guest appearances" over the years, thank you for sharing your many gifts and for bringing the humanizing influence of the arts into our business school classes. For the past decade, during the best and worst of times, this group of incredible human beings has been not just my team, but my tribe, my home, and my playground at work.

I am indebted to my senior associate deans and their staffs, who have supported me since the beginning in my efforts to build something costly that I figured would be fun and hoped would be useful. Glenn Carroll took the first and perhaps biggest risk, by giving me the time, space, permission, and money to bring in an acting teacher when the payoff for his investment was uncertain. Madhav Rajan and Yossi Feinberg stepped up the resources as the course grew and helped me to build a first-rate teaching team. And way back, before the course was a glimmer in anyone's eye, David Kreps created the context that sparked the whole thing, by nudging me into a class with Barbara Lanebrown, who opened my eyes to the value of an actor's mindset beyond the performing-arts world. Paul Mattish deserves special mention and degree-of-difficulty points for handling the logistics, from those first days in a trailer (there were no flat classrooms inside the building) to staffing five sections with thirteen temporary employees, wrangling performance and coaching spaces, building a living, growing inventory of plays and scenes, and making it all look easy.

The writing has involved another ensemble. My agent Christy Fletcher deserves enormous credit for grasping the first thread and pulling on it, for helping me craft (and sell) a successful book proposal, talking me down off a couple of ledges, calling in reinforcements, running interference, leading me gently in the right direction, and continuing to add tremendous value every time she weighs in. Talia Krohn, my gifted editor at Crown Publishing Group, has been so much more than that. She has been a spirit guide, materializing exactly when and how I needed, and helping to hack a clear path through the tangled vines of what is true and important to me and what needs to be said on the page. I had no right to expect such an invested, hardworking, and sage partner in this endeavor, not to mention one who would prove to be a joy to work with even during the heavy lifting. I am grateful to Peter Guzzardi and Melanie Rehak, who swept in when my wheels were spinning and got me unstuck, and whose voices, words, and turns of phrase will ring in my ears forever. Thanks to Bridget Samburg, who dug up some great anecdotes from parts of the world I don't inhabit. And thank you, Tina

Constable at the Crown Publishing Group, Helen Conford at Profile, and my other publishers across the globe for believing in me and in this book.

Sheryl Sandberg read an early draft and got me on the phone from the other side of the world, where she offered detailed comments, suggestions, support, and a good talking-to. A simple "like" emoji over email would have thrilled me. But instead, she was candid, intelligent, and spot on, and her input was transformative. Benoit Monin, my Stanford colleague (who is also a professional actor, an inspired social psychologist, my Acting with Power co-instructor, and my research collaborator), offered generous comments. He brought his Renaissance-homme, je-ne-sais-quoi sensibility to an early draft and improved it, greatly, in ways that I did not expect. Em Reit and the Saloner sisters read early drafts and offered input that was not only helpful but kind.

My thinking about power has been inspired by those who came before me. Some I have never met, such as Simone de Beauvoir, David McClelland, Hans Morgenthau, Serge Moscovici, and Martha Nussbaum, and others I have, such as David Kipnis, Charlan Nemeth, Jeffrey Pfeffer, Philip Tetlock, David Winter, and Philip Zimbardo. I have also been blessed with an incredible cadre of academic co-authors who have affected me immeasurably. Cameron Anderson, Nate Fast, Adam Galinsky, Lucia Guillory, Li Huang, Ena Inesi, Dacher Keltner, Michael Kraus, Katie Liljenquist, Joe Magee, Kim Rios Morrison, Em Reit, Niro Sivanathan, Melissa Thomas-Hunt, Larissa Tiedens, Jennifer Whitson, and Melissa Williams have all advanced my understanding of the challenges, so central to this book, of having power while feeling powerless, and of acting while in a position of power. My early work on group dynamics and interactions more broadly has also informed my writing here, thanks to the great minds of Holly Arrow, Ryan Beasley, Jennifer Berdahl, Elliot Fan, Andrea Hollingshead, Juliet Kaarbo, Peter Kim, Beta Mannix,

Paul Martorana, Joe McGrath, Maggie Neale, Kathleen O'Connor, Kathy Phillips, Jared Preston, and Bob Wyer. My students in MBA and executive education classes, past and present, far and wide, have taught me a lot about how power works in the real world and what it means to commit to something greater than yourself. I am especially grateful to those who have pressed me for answers I didn't have. And I am awed, truly, by the many people who have shared their incredible, inspiring, personally revealing, and validating stories with me. Some of you knew your story might end up in this book, others had no idea (and I've done my best to conceal your identities). Thank you for opening up and for inviting me, and all of us, to learn from your experience.

And now, for the dessert, because I've saved the best for last. To India and Dayssi, who are my reason for everything, I know it has not always felt that way. You inspire me daily with your grace, intelligence, heart, and humor; your formidable strengths; your resilience; and a maturity beyond your years. Thank you for your patience, for believing in me, and for wanting me to succeed. To my four parents and my sister, I love you and I admire you. I hope I have made you proud. You might not see yourselves in this book, but I thought about you, and us, every day while writing it. And to Garth, my partner in all things, all I can say is, you deserve a medal. Thank you for your bold, inspiring, and beneficent use of power, your steadfast support of the high-performing women in your life, and your inspirational commitment to the roles you play on every stage you inhabit.

Notes

Chapter 1: The Truth About Power

33 **One large meta-analysis showed:** S. C. Paustian-Underdahl, L. S. Walker, and D. J. Woehr, "Gender and Perceptions of Leadership Effectiveness: A Meta-Analysis of Contextual Moderators," *Journal of Applied Psychology* (April 28, 2014), advance online publication, http://dx.doi.org/10.1037/00036751.

Chapter 2: The Art and Science of Playing Power Up

42 *status play:* Keith Johnstone, *IMPRO: Improvisation and the Theatre* (London: Faber and Faber, 1979).

48 **belie respect and affection:** Dacher Keltner, Randall C. Young, Erin A. Heerey, Carmen Oemig, and Natalie D. Monarch, "Teasing in Hierarchical and Intimate Relations," *Journal of Personality and Social Psychology* 75 (1998): 1231–1247.

55 **"authority balance beam":** Richard J. Hackman and Diane Coutu, "Why Teams Don't Work," *Harvard Business Review* 87, no. 5 (2009): 98–105.

56 **the status of overconfident members was not damaged:** Cameron Anderson, Sebastien Brion, Don Moore, and Jessica A. Kennedy, "A Status Enhancement Account of Overconfidence," *Journal of Personality and Social Psychology* 103 (2012): 718–735.

Chapter 3: The Art and Science of Playing Power Down

70 **"show people the human side of you":** Howard Schultz and Adam Bryant, "Good C.E.O.s Are Insecure (and Know It)," *New York Times,* October 9, 2010.

73 **Their employees saw them as fickle and unpredictable:** David C. McClelland and David H. Burnham, "Power Is the Great Motivator," *Harvard Business Review,* January 2003.

76   **being likely to succeed:** Joey T. Cheng, Jessica L. Tracy, Tom Foulsham, Alan Kingstone, and Joseph Henrich, "Two Ways to the Top: Evidence That Dominance and Prestige Are Distinct Yet Viable Avenues to Social Rank and Influence," *Journal of Personality and Social Psychology* 104 (2013): 103–125.

77   **"expressed both positive emotion and anxiety, and used human words":** Ari Decter-Frain and Jeremy A. Frimer, "Impressive Words: Linguistic Predictors of Public Approval of the U.S. Congress," *Frontiers in Psychology* 7 (2016): 240, doi:10.3389/fpsyg.2016.00240.

77   **more on authoritativeness than the alternative:** Victor H. Vroom and Arthur G. Jago, "The Role of the Situation in Leadership," *American Psychologist* 62, no. 1 (January 2007): 17–24.

Chapter 4: Getting in Character

84   **"Being oneself," in other words, is an act:** Erving Goffman, *The Presentation of Self in Everyday Life* (New York: Anchor Books, 1959).

89   **last-born or only children:** David C. McClelland, *Human Motivation* (Cambridge University Press, 1988).

90   **women were more likely to repay the loans than men were:** Derek Thompson, "Women Are More Responsible with Money, Studies Show," *The Atlantic,* January 31, 2011.

93   **the two became close colleagues:** Brian Uzzi and Shannon Dunlap, "Make Your Enemies Your Allies," *Harvard Business Review,* May 2012.

93   **"truth or mission or love":** David Brooks, "Making Modern Toughness," *New York Times,* August 30, 2016, https://www.nytimes.com/2016/08/30/opinion/making-modern-toughness.html.

107   **describes how she was taught:** Herminia Ibarra, *Act Like a Leader, Think Like a Leader* (Boston: Harvard Business Review Press, 2015).

Chapter 5: Riding Shotgun

117   **upsets the old way of doing things:** National Research Council, *Sociality, Hierarchy, Health: Comparative Biodemography: A Collection of Papers,* edited by Maxine Weinstein and Meredith A. Lane (Washington, D.C.: National Academies Press, 2014).

118   **rising in the ranks was a priority at work:** Delroy L. Paulhus and Oliver P. John, "Egoistic and Moralistic Biases in Self-Perception: The Interplay of Self-Deceptive Styles with Basic Traits and Motives," *Journal of Personality* 66, no. 6 (1998): 1025–1060.

Chapter 6: The Show Must Go On

139 **"I was just, like, in shock":** "Jay-Z: The *Fresh Air* Interview," November 16, 2010, https://www.npr.org/2010/11/16/131334322/the-fresh -air-interview-jay-z-decoded.

140 **she became incapable of singing:** Amanda Petrusich, "A Transcendent Patti Smith Accepts Bob Dylan's Nobel Prize," *New Yorker,* December 10, 2016.

140 **"The opening chords of the song":** Patti Smith, "How Does It Feel?," *New Yorker,* December 14, 2016.

142 **would rather rank second than first:** Cameron Anderson, Robb Willer, Gavin J. Kilduff, and Courtney E. Brown, "The Origins of Deference: When Do People Prefer Lower Status?," *Journal of Personality and Social Psychology* 102, no. 5 (2012): 1077–88.

144 **the insiders were out to get him:** David Winter and Leslie A. Carlson, "Using Motive Scores in the Psychobiographical Study of an Individual: The Case of Richard Nixon," *Journal of Personality* 56, no. 1 (1988): 75–103.

Chapter 7: When Power Corrupts (and When It Doesn't)

161 **"I had lost the plot":** Jonathan Shieber, "500 Startups' Dave McClure Apologizes for 'Multiple' Advances toward Women and Being a 'Creep,'" *TechCrunch,* July 1, 2017.

163 **increased their appetites or undermined their capacity to control them:** Dacher Keltner, "Don't Let Power Corrupt You," *Harvard Business Review,* October 2016.

166 **more likely to retaliate professionally against the subordinate:** Melissa J. Williams, Deborah H Gruenfeld, and Lucia E. Guillory, "Sexual Aggression When Power Is New: Effects of Acute High Power on Chronically Low-Power Individuals," *Journal of Personality and Social Psychology* 112, no. 2 (2017): 201–223.

169 **"the branches are control":** Lundy Bancroft, *Why Does He Do That?* (New York: Putnam, 2002).

169 **it is not always clear who is who:** Cavan Sieczkowski, "Former CIA Officer: Listen to Your Enemy, Because 'Everybody Believes They Are the Good Guy,'" *Huffington Post,* June 14, 2016.

171 **his father's gambling addiction:** Nina Munk, "Steve Wynn's Biggest Battle," *Vanity Fair,* June 2005.

173 **she was finally indicted for fraud:** John Carreyrou, *Bad Blood* (New York: Knopf, 2018).

174 **"ended up getting Kalancik fired":** Stanford Graduate School of Business, December 3, 2018; video on YouTube.

177 **"you keep looking in all the wrong places for the parent who abused you":** Lucinda Franks, "The Intimate History," *Talk Magazine,* September 1999.

178 **more likely to call her later and ask her out:** Donald G. Dutton and Arthur P. Aron, "Some Evidence for Heightened Sexual Attraction under Conditions of High Anxiety," *Journal of Personality and Social Psychology* 30 (1974): 510–517.

Chapter 8: How to Wrangle a Bully

192 **while verbal assertiveness or dominance:** M. J. Williams and L. Z. Tiedens, "The Subtle Suspension of Backlash: A Meta-analysis of Penalties for Women's Implicit and Explicit Dominance Behavior," *Psychological Bulletin* 142, no. 2 (2016): 165–197.

Chapter 9: The Bystander Role and New Ways to Play It

198 **garnering almost a million views:** Jim Dwyer, "When Fists and Kicks Fly on the Subway, It's Snackman to the Rescue," *New York Times,* April 12, 2012.

209 **"when the guys they admire most are already there":** Shelley Correll, "Reducing Gender Biases in Modern Workplaces: A Small Wins Approach to Organizational Change," *Gender and Society,* November 9, 2017.

Chapter 10: How to Use Power While Playing the Lead

219 **"do a better job on that":** National Public Radio, "Paul Ryan's Full Interview with NPR's Steve Inskeep," December 1, 2017, https://www.npr.org/2017/12/01/567012522/.

226 **less evident in those who feel more needy:** George Kohlrieser, "Secure Base Leadership: What It Means and Why It Really Matters," *Talent and Management,* October 23, 2012.

233 **"because no chief executive . . . requires full surrender":** Rakesh Khurana, "The Curse of the Superstar CEO," *Harvard Business Review,* September 2002, https://hbr.org/2002/09/the-curse-of-the-superstar-ceo.

235 **choices between individual and group payoffs:** N. Halevy, E. Y. Chou, T. R. Cohen, and R. W. Livingston, "Status Conferral in Intergroup Social Dilemmas: Behavioral Antecedents and Consequences of Prestige and Dominance," *Journal of Personality and Social Psychology* 102, no. 2 (2012): 351–366, http://dx.doi.org/10.1037/a0025515.

Index